Master .NET Fundamentals

Learn Core Concepts, Optimize Your Preparation, Nail the Interview Process, and Secure Your Dream Job in Tech

Nirbhay Chauhan

About the Author

Nirbhay Chauhan Author of "Master .NET Fundamentals"

Nirbhay Chauhan is a passionate software developer with a deep understanding of the .NET landscape. His journey began in 2000, diving headfirst into the world of computers with DOS and programming languages like C and FoxPro. This early exposure ignited a lifelong love of technology and problem-solving.

Nirbhay's career took a pivotal turn in 2009 when he achieved the coveted SCJP certification, solidifying his grasp of Java programming. But the following year, in 2010, he discovered his true calling: .NET development. This shift opened doors to exciting opportunities with various multinational corporations, both product-based and service-based.

Over the past 14 years, Nirbhay has honed his skills in a vast array of .NET technologies, including ASP.NET, C#, VB.NET, Web Forms, Win Forms, WPF, WCF, .NET Core, and SQL. His experience extends beyond coding, encompassing the successful migration of legacy applications to modern .NET frameworks. He's also played a key role in designing and architecting numerous desktop and web applications.

Nirbhay's passion extends far beyond his own expertise. He actively participates in the .NET developer community, giving and taking interviews, and even training aspiring developers eager to excel in this dynamic field. Driven by the motto "Life is teaching and I'm still learning," Nirbhay is a lifelong learner who thrives on sharing his knowledge. This zeal to connect with aspiring developers led him to create the popular YouTube channel "@DotNetInterviewCommunity," a valuable resource for anyone seeking to ace their .NET job interview.

With his extensive experience, practical knowledge, and dedication to empowering others, Nirbhay Chauhan is the ideal guide to help you navigate the .NET interview process with confidence. Let his insights in the ".NET Interview Preparation" book be your key to unlocking your dream .NET career.

Connect the author at: nirbhaychauhan2015@gmail.com

Share your story and questions to help us all learn and grow together. Join us at: https://www.youtube.com/@dotnetinterviewcommunity

Why You Should Read "Master .NET Fundamentals "

Are you a .NET developer looking to take your career to the next level? If so, then you need to read "Master .NET Fundamentals ." This comprehensive guide is your one-stop shop for mastering the essential concepts and skills required to ace your .NET interviews.

Here's why you should read this book:

- **Comprehensive Coverage:** This book covers a wide range of topics, including software development life cycle, software development principles, .NET Framework history, .NET Framework, design patterns, exception handling, Microsoft SQL Server, and resume preparation.
- **Structured Approach:** The book is organized in a logical and easy-to-follow manner, making it simple to understand and retain the information.
- **Practical Advice:** Throughout the book, you'll find practical advice and tips that will help you apply the concepts you learn to real-world interview questions.
- **Time-Saving:** By reading this book, you can save yourself the time and frustration of searching for information online and trying to organize your notes.
- **Digital Detox:** This physical book is a great alternative to spending hours in front of a computer screen, allowing you to study more comfortably and efficiently.

Whether you're a beginner or an experienced .NET developer, this book is a valuable resource that will help you achieve your career goals. Don't miss out on this opportunity to level up your .NET skills and land your dream job.

LIMITS OF LIABILITY/DISCLAIMER OF WARRANTY

CONTENTS

Introduction: Your Path to .NET Interview Success

Are you a .NET developer feeling overwhelmed by the sheer volume of information available online to prepare for interviews? Have you struggled to find a reliable source of questions and answers that truly reflect the challenges you'll face in real-world interviews?

I've been there myself. When I was preparing for my own .NET interviews, I found myself lost in a sea of blog posts, tutorials, and forums. It was incredibly difficult to determine which resources were truly valuable and which were just noise. I spent countless hours bookmarking articles and trying to organise my notes, but it was a never-ending battle.

And let's not forget the pain of trying to find that one article you read weeks ago. Revisiting information online can be a time-consuming and frustrating process.

I knew there had to be a better way. A more structured, comprehensive approach that would equip me with the knowledge and confidence to ace any .NET interview. So, I embarked on a journey to create a collection of interview questions and answers. I poured over countless resources, analysed past interview experiences, and distilled the most essential concepts into a cohesive framework.

The result is this book, "Master .NET Fundamentals". It's not just a collection of questions; it's a roadmap to your .NET interview success. Each chapter is designed to provide you with a deep understanding of the core concepts and technologies that are essential for .NET developers.

From the software development life cycle to design patterns and database interactions, this book covers everything you need to know.

But this book offers more than just content. It's a solution to the constant struggle of finding and revisiting information online. With this book, you have all the essential knowledge at your fingertips, ready to be reviewed whenever you need it.

Additionally, in an age of digital detox, this book provides a much-needed respite from screen time. Instead of straining your eyes in front of a computer or mobile device, you can simply pick up this physical book and start studying.

By addressing these common pain points, this book offers a win-win solution for aspiring .NET developers. It provides a comprehensive resource, eliminates the frustration of searching for information online, and promotes a healthier work-life balance.

CHAPTER 1

SOFTWARE DEVELOPMENT AND LIFE CYCLE

What is the Software Development?

Software Development is the process of transforming a problem or need into a computer-based solution. Software development is a collaborative process involving:

Problem Identification: Identifying the issue that needs a software solution.

Requirement Gathering: Understanding the exact needs and expectations of users.

Design: Creating a blueprint of the software's architecture or UI/UX and functionality.

Coding: Writing the actual code using programming languages.

Testing: Ensuring the software works as intended and identifying bugs.

Deployment: Releasing the software to users.

Maintenance: Updating and fixing issues in the software over time.

How many Types of Software are there?

There are many software applications present, however, mainly these software can be categorized into two main types:

1. **System Software**: It's like the brain behind your computer. It's the software that tells your computer's hardware what to do. System software takes the commands you give to your computer and turns them into something the computer hardware can understand and perform an action.

2. **Application Software**: It's like the tools in your toolbox. They're the programs you use to get things done on your computer. Think of word processors for writing, spreadsheets for calculations, or games for fun. Unlike system software, which runs the computer itself, application software helps you work, create, or entertain yourself.

Is Programming Software an Application Software?

Yes, Programming Software is also an application software, as it helps programmers perform specific tasks such as coding, debugging, and other activities. Examples of programming software are Visual Studio, Eclipse, etc.

What are the Types of Software Development?

Software development is like a versatile tool kit. It offers a variety of approaches and techniques to build different kinds of software, each tailored to specific needs. Below are some of the types of software development:

1. Web Application Development

2. Desktop Application Development

3. Mobile Application Development

4. Game Development

5. Enterprise Application Development
6. Embedded System Development
7. Blockchain Development
8. Cloud Computing
9. Cyber Security
10. Artificial Intelligence

What is the Software Development Process?

The software development process is the roadmap for creating software. It's a series of steps that guides a team or teams from an initial idea to a finished product.

What Steps are involved in the Software Development Process?

The software development process typically involves these key stages:

1. **Planning and Requirements Gathering:** Understanding the problem, defining the software's purpose, and identifying user needs.
2. **Design:** Creating a blueprint of the software, including its architecture, user interface, and functionality. This involves:
   - Architectural design: Defining the overall structure.
   - Detailed design: Specifying how components will interact.
3. **Development:** Writing the code to bring the design to life. This includes:
   - Coding: Writing the software's codebase.
   - Code reviews: Ensuring code quality and adherence to standards.

   - Version control: Tracking changes to the code.

4. **Testing:** Checking the software for errors and ensuring it meets requirements. This includes:
   - Unit testing: Testing individual components.
   - System testing: Testing the entire system.
   - Manual testing: Human testers interact with the software.
   - Automated testing: Using software to perform tests.
5. **Deployment:** Releasing the software to users. This involves:
   - Release planning: Determining the release date and strategy.
   - Deployment automation: Using tools to automate the deployment process.
6. **Maintenance:** Providing ongoing support, updates, and bug fixes. This includes gathering user feedback to improve the software.

What is Software Development Lifecycle or SDLC?

SDLC stands for **Software Development Lifecycle**. It's a structured process that outlines the steps involved in creating, testing, and deploying software. It's like a roadmap that guides software development teams from the initial concept to the final product.

The SDLC typically involves these key phases/stages:

- **Planning and Requirements Gathering:** Understanding the software's purpose and identifying user needs.
- **Design:** Creating a blueprint of the software's structure and functionality.
- **Development:** Writing the code to bring the design to life.
- **Testing:** Checking the software for errors and ensuring it meets

requirements.

- **Deployment:** Releasing the software to users.
- **Maintenance:** Providing ongoing support, updates, and bug fixes.

By following these steps, software development teams and software-creating organizations can create high-quality software efficiently and effectively.

What are the Software Development Lifecycle (SDLC) Models?

SDLC models are frameworks that outline the various stages involved in developing software. Each model has its strengths and weaknesses, and the best choice depends on the project's specific requirements.

Explain some of the different types of Software Development Lifecycle (SDLC) Models.

Below are some of the commonly used Software Development Lifecycle (SDLC) Models:

Traditional Models:

- Waterfall Model: A linear sequential design process where each phase depends on the deliverables of the previous one.
- V-Shaped Model: An extension of the Waterfall model with emphasis on testing at each stage.

Iterative Models:

- Iterative Model: Development occurs in iterative cycles, allowing for refinements based on feedback.
- Incremental Model: The software is built in increments, with each increment delivering a functional part of the system.
- Spiral Model: Combines iterative development with risk

analysis.

Agile Models:

- Agile Model: Emphasizes flexibility, collaboration, and iterative development.
- Scrum: A popular Agile framework focusing on sprints and cross-functional teams.
- Kanban: A visual method for managing work and improving flow.

Other Models:

- Prototype Model: Creating a prototype for user feedback before full development.
- RAD Model: Rapid Application Development Model prioritizes speed and flexibility.

What is the Rapid Application Development (RAD) Model?

Rapid Application Development (RAD) is a software development methodology that prioritizes speed and flexibility. It emphasizes rapid prototyping and iterative development over extensive planning and documentation.

Key characteristics of RAD:

- **Focus on prototyping**: Creating functional models of the software early in the development process.
- **Iterative development**: Building the software in small, incremental stages with continuous feedback.
- **Reusability**: Utilizing pre-built components to accelerate development.
- **Active user involvement**: Constant collaboration with end-users to ensure the product meets their needs.

RAD is ideal for projects with:

- Clearly defined requirements.
- A skilled development team.
- A need for rapid time-to-market.

By emphasizing speed, flexibility, and user involvement, RAD helps organizations deliver software solutions quickly and efficiently.

Why is RAD not very popular? Or What are the drawbacks of RAD?

While RAD offers several advantages, it's not suitable for every project. Here are some of its drawbacks:

- **Requires Highly Skilled Teams**: RAD relies heavily on experienced developers and designers who can work efficiently under pressure.
- **Limited System Complexity**: Complex systems may be difficult to develop using RAD due to its focus on speed.
- **Dependency on Strong Developer-Customer Relationship**: Continuous involvement and feedback from the customer are essential, which can be challenging to maintain.
- **Potential for Technical Debt**: Rapid development might lead to shortcuts, resulting in technical debt that can be costly to address later.
- **Documentation Challenges**: The focus on speed might lead to inadequate documentation, which can be problematic for future maintenance.
- **Scalability Issues**: RAD might not be suitable for large-scale systems that require extensive planning and design.

What is the Agile Software Development Model?

Agile is a dynamic approach to software development that prioritizes flexibility, collaboration, and rapid delivery. Unlike traditional methods, Agile breaks down projects into smaller, manageable chunks called sprints. This iterative process allows teams to adapt to changing requirements and deliver value incrementally.

Key principles of Agile:

- Individuals and interactions over processes and tools
- Working software over comprehensive documentation
- Customer collaboration over contract negotiation
- Responding to change by following a plan

Popular Agile frameworks:

Agile offers a variety of frameworks to suit different project needs and team preferences. Here are some of the most widely used:

- Scrum: Often considered the most popular Agile framework, Scrum emphasizes teamwork, accountability, and iterative development.
- Kanban: Focuses on visualizing workflow and continuously improving processes.
- Extreme Programming (XP): Emphasizes simplicity, communication, feedback, and courage.
- Feature-Driven Development (FDD): Centers around delivering client-valued features.
- Lean Software Development: Applies Lean principles to software development, focusing on eliminating waste.

What are the Principles of Agile Software Development Methodology?

Below are the Principles of Agile Software Development:

Agile development is built on a set of guiding principles that prioritize people, collaboration, and delivering value. Here are some key ideas:

- Focus on people: Agile believes in empowering individuals and teams. It's about creating an environment where people can thrive and contribute their best.

- Deliver value early and often: Instead of waiting for a big, perfect product, Agile teams deliver working software in small, incremental steps. This allows for constant feedback and improvement.

- Embrace change: The world is always changing, and Agile recognizes this. It encourages teams to be flexible and adapt to new information.

- Collaboration is key: Agile teams work closely together, sharing ideas and knowledge. This open communication leads to better solutions.

- Continuous improvement: Agile is about getting better over time. Teams regularly reflect on their work and find ways to improve their processes.

These principles work together to create a dynamic and effective approach to software development.

What are the Core Values of Agile Software Development?

There are 4 Core Agile Values: The Heart of Agile Development

Agile is all about working smarter, not harder. It's based on four simple but powerful ideas:

1. **People over processes**: Agile believes that the people working

on a project are more important than the rules or steps they follow. It's about teamwork and using people's skills to solve problems.

2. **Working software over paperwork**: Instead of spending lots of time writing about the software, Agile teams focus on actually building and delivering something useful.

3. **Customer collaboration over contracts**: Agile teams work closely with their customers to understand their needs and make sure the software is what they really want.

4. **Responding to change over following a plan**: Things change, and Agile is about being ready for that. Instead of sticking to a rigid plan, Agile teams can adjust their work as needed to deliver the best possible product.

These values help Agile teams create better software, faster.

How Companies Use Agile Software Development Methodology?

Companies use Agile to build software more flexibly and efficiently.

- **Breaking it down**: Big projects are divided into smaller, more manageable chunks called sprints.
- **Working together**: Teams work closely with each other and with customers to understand what needs to be done.
- **Trying it out**: Instead of waiting to finish everything, Agile teams create a working version of the software early on and improve it based on feedback.
- **Staying flexible**: Plans can change, and that's okay in Agile. Teams can adjust their work as needed to meet new challenges.
- **Continuous improvement**: Agile teams always look for ways to work better. They learn from their mistakes and try new things.

By following these steps, companies can build software faster, with fewer mistakes, and that people love to use.

What is SAFe? and Is it an Agile Framework?

Yes, SAFe (Scaled Agile Framework) is an agile framework. However, it's specifically designed for scaling Agile principles to larger organizations and complex projects. Unlike traditional Agile frameworks like Scrum or Kanban, which focus on individual teams, SAFe provides a structure for aligning and coordinating multiple Agile teams within an enterprise.

SAFe incorporates elements of Scrum, Kanban, and other Agile practices but extends them to address the challenges of large-scale development.

Chapter 2

Software Development Principles

What are the Software Development Principles?

Software development principles are the guiding lights for creating efficient, reliable, and maintainable software. While there are numerous principles, here are some of the most fundamental ones:

General Software Development Principles:

- **Modularity**: Breaking down software into smaller, independent components.
- **Abstraction**: Focusing on essential features while hiding implementation details.
- **Encapsulation**: Combining data and methods that operate on that data into a single unit.
- **Information Hiding**: Protecting data from unauthorized access.
- **Coupling**: Measuring the degree of dependency between software components.
- **Cohesion**: Measuring the degree to which elements within a module belong together.

- **KISS (Keep It Simple, Stupid)**: Creating software that is easy to understand and maintain.
- **DRY (Don't Repeat Yourself)**: Avoiding code duplication.
- **YAGNI (You Aren't Going To Need It):** Avoiding premature optimization.

Design Principles:

- **SOLID**: A set of five design principles for creating maintainable object-oriented software (Single Responsibility, Open-Closed, Liskov Substitution, Interface Segregation, Dependency Inversion).
- **GRASP**: A set of object-oriented design patterns.

Agile Principles:

- **Customer Satisfaction**: Delivering value early and continuously.
- **Embrace Change**: Adapting to changing requirements.
- **Frequent Delivery**: Delivering working software frequently.
- **Collaboration**: Close cooperation between business and development teams.
- **Individual Motivation**: Empowering individuals.
- **Face-to-Face Communication**: Effective communication through in-person interactions.
- **Working Software**: Measuring progress by working software.
- **Sustainable Pace**: Maintaining a steady development pace.
- **Technical Excellence**: Focus on quality and good design.
- **Simplicity**: Avoiding unnecessary complexity.

- **Self-Organizing Teams**: Empowering teams to make decisions.
- **Regular Reflection**: Continuously improving processes.

Additional Principles:

- **Reliability**: Software should perform its intended functions without failure.
- **Efficiency**: Software should use system resources judiciously.
- **Maintainability**: Software should be easy to understand, test, and modify.
- **Usability**: Software should be easy to learn and use.
- **Portability**: Software should be able to run on different hardware or software platforms.
- **Security**: Software should protect data and systems from unauthorized access.

These principles provide a foundation for creating robust, efficient, and user-friendly software systems.

Explain the GRASP Principle.

GRASP stands for General Responsibility Assignment Software Patterns. It's a set of principles that help developers make informed decisions about assigning responsibilities to objects within an object-oriented system.

Important GRASP Patterns:

- **Information Expert**: Assign a responsibility to the class that has the information needed to fulfill it. For instance, a Customer class would be responsible for calculating its total purchases.

- **Creator**: Assign the responsibility of creating an object to a class that:
  - Contains or aggregates instances of the created class.
  - Has the information to initialize the created object.
  - Uses the created object.
- **Controller**: Assign the responsibility of handling a system operation to a class representing the overall system or a use case scenario.
- **Low Coupling**: Design classes with minimal dependencies on other classes.
- **High Cohesion**: Keep related responsibilities within a single class.
- **Polymorphism**: Assign responsibility to several classes based on type variations.
- **Pure Fabrication**: Introduce a new class to take on responsibilities that don't naturally fit anywhere else.
- **Indirection**: Use an intermediate object to decouple objects that need to communicate.
- **Protected Variations**: Identify points of expected variation and encapsulate them.

The **Information Expert pattern** suggests assigning a responsibility to the class that has the information necessary to fulfill that responsibility. In essence, the class that knows the most about something should be responsible for handling it.

C# Example: Order and OrderItem

Consider an e-commerce system with Order and OrderItem classes. An Order consists of multiple OrderItems.

public class OrderItem

```
{
    public int Quantity { get; set; }
    public decimal Price { get; set; }
    public decimal GetTotalPrice() => Quantity * Price;
}
public class Order
{
    public List<OrderItem> Items { get; set; } = new();
    public decimal CalculateTotal()
    {
        return Items.Sum(item => item.GetTotalPrice());
    }
}
```

In this example:

OrderItem knows its quantity and price, so it's responsible for calculating its total price (Information Expert).

Order knows its items, so it's responsible for calculating the total order price (Information Expert).

By following Information Expert, we've created a clear separation of responsibilities, making the code more understandable and maintainable.

The **Creator pattern** in GRASP suggests assigning the responsibility of creating an object to a class that:

- Contains or aggregates instances of the created class.
- Records instances of the created class.

- Closely uses instances of the created class.
- Has the information for initializing the created object.

C# Example: Order and OrderItem

Let's expand on the previous Order and OrderItem example to illustrate the Creator pattern:

```
public class OrderFactory
{
    public Order CreateOrder(List<OrderItem> items)
    {
        return new Order { Items = items };
    }
}
```

In this example:

- OrderFactory is responsible for creating Order objects.
- It encapsulates the logic for creating an order based on a list of order items.
- By introducing an OrderFactory, we've separated the responsibility of creating an Order from the Order class itself. This improves modularity and flexibility.

The **Controller pattern** in GRASP assigns the responsibility of handling system events to a non-UI class that represents the overall system or a use case scenario. Essentially, the controller acts as a mediator between the user interface and the domain layer.

C# Example: Order Processing

Consider a simple e-commerce application. A user clicks a "Place Order" button. The controller would be responsible for handling this event:

```
public class OrderController

{

   private readonly OrderService _orderService;

   public OrderController(OrderService orderService)

   {

      _orderService = orderService;

   }

   public

void PlaceOrder(List<OrderItem> items)

   {

      var order = _orderService.CreateOrder(items);

      // Additional logic, such as sending order confirmation, updating
inventory, etc.

   }

}
```

In this example:

- The OrderController handles the "Place Order" event.
- It delegates the order creation logic to the OrderService (which might be another layer of abstraction).
- It can perform additional actions related to the order

placement, such as sending notifications or updating inventory.

Key Points:

- The controller is not part of the domain model but coordinates the flow of data and logic.
- It helps to separate the UI from the business logic.
- It can handle multiple use cases.

By using the Controller pattern, we achieve a cleaner separation of concerns and improve the overall structure of the application.

Low Coupling is a fundamental principle in object-oriented design that aims to minimize dependencies between classes. When classes are tightly coupled, changes to one class can have ripple effects on others, making the system harder to maintain and test.

Achieving Low Coupling:

- Dependency Injection: Injecting dependencies rather than creating them within a class.
- Interfaces: Using interfaces to decouple implementations from clients.
- Event-Based Communication: Using events to decouple components.
- Layered Architecture: Organizing code into layers with clear dependencies.

C# Example:

```
public interface IOrderServcie

{

    void SaveOrder(Order order);
```

```
}

public class OrderService

{

   private readonly IOrderService _orderService;

   public OrderService(IOrderService orderServ)

   {

      _orderService = orderServ;

   }

public void PlaceOrder(Order order)

   {

      // ... order processing logic

      _orderService.SaveOrder(order);

   }

}
```

In this example:

OrderService depends on the IOrderService interface, not a specific implementation.

This allows for easy substitution of different repository implementations without affecting OrderService.

By adhering to low coupling, you create more flexible, maintainable, and testable software.

High cohesion means that a class or module should have a clear, focused responsibility. In simpler terms, everything within a class should be closely related to its primary purpose.

Benefits of high cohesion:

- **Improved readability**: Code is easier to understand when it's focused on a single task.
- **Increased maintainability**: Changes to one part of the class are less likely to affect other parts.
- **Enhanced reusability**: Classes with high cohesion are more likely to be reusable in different parts of the application.

Example:

A Customer class should primarily contain customer-related data and methods (e.g., name, address, order history). It shouldn't also handle database interactions or user interface logic.

By striving for high cohesion, you create software that is easier to maintain, understand, and modify.

What is the relationship between high cohesion and low coupling?

High cohesion and low coupling are two sides of the same coin when designing well-structured software.

High cohesion means that the elements within a module are closely related and focused on a single task.

Low coupling means that modules are independent, and changes in one module have minimal impact on others.

When combined, they create software that is:

- **Easier to understand**: Code is more organized and focused.
- **More maintainable**: Changes are less likely to have unintended consequences.

- **More testable**: Individual components can be tested in isolation.
- **More reusable**: Well-defined modules can be used in different parts of the application.

Example:

Imagine a car. The engine (high cohesion) is responsible for generating power. It has minimal interaction with the wheels (low coupling), allowing independent changes to either component.

How can we achieve High Cohesion and Low Coupling?

Techniques for High Cohesion:

- **Single Responsibility Principle (SRP)**: Each class should have one responsibility.
- **Identify Related Functions**: Group closely related functions within a class.
- **Avoid God Objects**: Prevent classes from taking on too many responsibilities.
- **Refactoring**: Continuously improve the code structure and eliminate redundancy.

Techniques for Low Coupling:

- **Dependency Injection**: Inject dependencies rather than creating them within a class.
- **Interfaces**: Define contracts between components.
- **Modularization**: Break down the system into independent modules.
- **Loose Coupling**: Minimize dependencies between modules.

- **Event-Based Architecture**: Decouple components using events.

Example:

Consider an e-commerce application:

High Cohesion: An Order class might contain properties like OrderId, TotalAmount, OrderDate, OrderItems, and methods related to Order information.

```
public class Order

{

  public int OrderId { get; set; }

  public decimal TotalAmount { get; set; }

  public DateTime OrderDate { get; set; }

  public List<OrderItem> OrderItems { get; set; } = new();

   public void CalculateTotal()

   {

     // Logic to calculate the total amount based on order items

   }

}
```

In this example, the Order class is highly cohesive because it encapsulates all the information and behavior related to an order. The CalculateTotal method further adds cohesion.

Low Coupling: The Product class should not directly interact with the database or user interface. Instead, use a repository or service layer to handle these interactions.

```
public interface IOrderService
```

```
{
  voidSaveOrder(Order order);
  Order GetOrderById(int orderId);
}
public class OrderService
{
  private readonly IOrderService _orderServcie;
  public OrderService(IOrderService orderServcie)
  {
    _orderServcie = orderServcie;
  }
  public void PlaceOrder(Order order)
  {
    // Business logic for placing order
    _orderServcie.SaveOrder(order);
  }
}
```

The OrderService depends on the IOrderServcie interface, not on any specific implementation.

This creates a loose coupling between the OrderService and the data access layer.

Explain refactoring techniques to improve cohesion and coupling in C# code.

Refactoring is the process of improving code without changing its external behavior. Here are some techniques to enhance cohesion and coupling:

Breaking Down Large Classes:

- **Extract Class**: Create a new class to encapsulate related data and behavior from an existing class.
- **Extract Interface**: Identify an interface that several classes implement to reduce coupling.
- **Extract Superclass**: Identify commonalities between classes and create a base class.

Simplifying Complex Logic

- **Introduce Explaining Variable**: Assign complex expressions to a meaningful variable.
- **Replace Temporary with Query**: Replace temporary variables with method calls or expressions.
- **Extract Method**: Extract a block of code into a separate method.

Managing Dependencies

- **Dependency Injection**: Inject dependencies through constructors or properties.
- **Dependency Inversion**: Use interfaces to decouple components.
- **Remove Middle Man**: Eliminate unnecessary intermediary objects.

Improving Cohesion

- **Combine Functions**: Merge closely related functions into a single method.
- **Move Method**: Relocate a method to a class where it more logically belongs.
- **Extract Class**: Create a new class to encapsulate related data and behavior.

Additional Considerations

Code Reviews: Regularly review code to identify areas for improvement.

Unit Testing: Write unit tests to verify the correctness of refactored code.

Incremental Changes: Refactor in small steps to avoid introducing new bugs.

Example:

Consider a Customer class with methods for calculating discounts, saving to a database, and sending emails. This violates the Single Responsibility Principle.

Refactoring:

Extract Class: Create a DiscountCalculator class to handle discount calculations.

Introduce Interface: Create an ICustomerDataService interface for data access.

Dependency Injection: Inject ICustomerDataService into the Customer class.

Explain the SOLID Principles.

SOLID is an acronym for five design principles that help in creating robust, maintainable, and scalable software applications. Let's understand each principle with C# examples.

S: Single Responsibility Principle (SRP): A class should have only one reason to change.

```
public class Order

{

  public int OrderId { get; set; }

  public decimal TotalAmount { get; set; }

  //Order properties and methods

}

public class OrderValidator

{

  public bool IsValid(Order order)

  {

    // Validation logic

  }

}
```

In this example, Order is responsible for order data, while OrderValidator is responsible for validation.

O: Open-Closed Principle (OCP): Objects should be open for extension but closed for modification.

```
public abstract class Shape
```

```
{
public abstract double CalculateArea();
}
public class Rectangle : Shape
{
public double Width { get; set; }
public double Height { get; set; }
public override double
CalculateArea() => Width * Height;
}
```

New shapes can be added by inheriting from Shape without modifying existing code.

L: Liskov Substitution Principle (LSP): Objects in a program should be replaceable with instances of their subtypes without altering the correctness of that program.

```
public abstract class Shape
{
  public abstract double CalculateArea();
}
public class Rectangle : Shape
{
  //...
}
public class Square : Rectangle
```

```
{
  public double Side { get; set; }
  public override double CalculateArea() => Side * Side;
}
```

A Square is a special type of Rectangle, so it should be substitutable without issues.

I: Interface Segregation Principle (ISP): Clients should not be forced to depend on methods they do not use.

```
public interface IPrinter
{
  voidPrintText(string text);
}
public interface IScanner
{
  string ScanDocument();
}
public class MultiFunctionDevice : IPrinter,IScanner
{
  //Implementation for both print and scan functions
}
```

Clients using only printing functionality can depend on IPrinter.

D: Dependency Inversion Principle (DIP): High-level modules should not depend on low-level modules. Both should depend on abstractions.

```
public interface IEmailService
```

```
{
   voidSendEmail(string to, string subject, string body);
}
 public class OrderService
{
   private readonly IEmailService _emailService;
   public OrderService(IEmailService emailService)
   {
      _emailService = emailService;
   }
}
```

OrderService depends on the IEmailService abstraction, not a concrete implementation.

By adhering to these SOLID principles, you can create more maintainable, flexible, and extensible software.

How to apply SOLID Principles in a larger project?

Applying **SOLID principles in large-scale projects** requires a systematic and collaborative approach. Here are some key strategies:

Project Initiation and Planning:

- **Identify Core Domains**: Break down the project into distinct domains or subsystems.
- **Apply SOLID at the Micro Level**: Ensure each component within a domain adheres to SOLID principles.
- **Define Clear Interfaces**: Establish well-defined interfaces

between components to promote loose coupling.

- **Choose Appropriate Design Patterns**: Select design patterns that align with SOLID principles.

Team Collaboration:

- **Code Reviews**: Conduct regular code reviews to enforce SOLID principles.
- **Shared Understanding**: Ensure the entire team understands SOLID principles and their importance.
- **Pair Programming**: Collaborate on code development to share knowledge and improve code quality.

Continuous Improvement

- **Refactoring**: Regularly refactor code to improve design and maintainability.
- **Code Metrics**: Use code metrics to identify potential violations of SOLID principles.
- **Design Patterns**: Apply appropriate design patterns to enhance code structure.

Additional Considerations

- **Test-Driven Development (TDD)**: Write tests before writing code to encourage SOLID design.
- **Dependency Injection**: Use dependency injection to manage dependencies effectively.
- **Domain-Driven Design (DDD)**: Model the problem domain using object-oriented principles.

Example: In a large e-commerce application:

Core Domains: Order processing, product catalog, customer management, payment processing.

SOLID Application: Each domain would have its own set of classes adhering to SOLID principles. For instance, the Order class would encapsulate order-related data and behavior, while the OrderProcessor class would handle order-processing logic.

Dependency Injection: Inject dependencies like ProductService, CustomerService, and PaymentService into the OrderProcessor to promote loose coupling.

What are the challenges of applying SOLID principles to large projects?

While SOLID principles are invaluable for building robust and maintainable software, applying them effectively in large-scale projects can be challenging. Here are some common hurdles:

1. Legacy Code:

- **Overcoming Existing Structure**: Many legacy systems need to adhere to SOLID principles. Refactoring to comply can take time and effort.
- **Balancing Refactoring with New Features**: Finding the right balance between improving code quality and delivering new functionalities.

2. Team Collaboration:

- **Consistent Application**: Ensuring all team members understand and apply SOLID principles consistently.
- **Knowledge Sharing**: Effectively communicating SOLID concepts and benefits to the entire team.

3. Performance Overhead:

- **Potential for Over-Engineering**: Overly strict adherence to SOLID can sometimes lead to performance issues.
- **Finding the Right Balance**: Balancing the benefits of SOLID with performance requirements.

4. Time Constraints:

- **Short Development Cycles**: Pressure to deliver quickly might lead to shortcuts and violations of SOLID principles.
- **Long-Term Benefits vs. Short-Term Deliverables**: Balancing immediate needs with the long-term advantages of SOLID.

5. Complexity:

- **Large Codebases**: Understanding the entire codebase to apply SOLID effectively can be overwhelming.
- **Identifying Dependencies**: Identifying and managing dependencies between components can be complex.

6. Cultural Challenges:

- **Resistance to Change**: Overcoming resistance to refactoring and adopting new approaches.
- **Prioritizing SOLID**: Balancing SOLID principles with other project priorities.

Overcoming these challenges requires a combination of careful planning, effective communication, and a commitment to long-term code quality.

What is the Programming Paradigm? Explain in detail

A programming paradigm is a fundamental style or programming approach that defines how you conceptualize and structure the implementation of a computer program. It's essentially a mental model that guides how you think about code and problem-solving.

Paradigms provide a framework for understanding how to build software, influencing the choice of programming languages, data structures, algorithms, and overall program design.

Key Programming Paradigms:

- **Imperative Programming**: This is the most common paradigm, focusing on describing the steps needed to achieve a result. Instructions are executed sequentially, modifying the program's state. Examples include C, Pascal, and early versions of Fortran.

- **Object-Oriented Programming (OOP)**: This paradigm revolves around the concept of objects, which encapsulate data (attributes) and behavior (methods). OOP emphasizes reusability and modularity. Examples include Java, C++, Python, and C#.

- **Functional Programming**: This paradigm treats computation as the evaluation of mathematical functions. It emphasizes immutability, pure functions, and higher-order functions. Examples include Haskell, Lisp, and F#.

- **Declarative Programming**: This paradigm focuses on describing the desired outcome rather than the steps to achieve it. SQL and HTML are common examples.

- **Logic Programming**: Based on mathematical logic, using rules and facts to solve problems. Prolog is a classic example.

Other Paradigms:

- **Structured Programming**: Emphasizes code readability and maintainability through control flow structures.

- **Generic Programming**: Creates reusable code components through templates or generics.
- **Aspect-Oriented Programming (AOP)**: Separates concerns into different modules.
- It's important to note that many programming languages support multiple paradigms, allowing for a mix of approaches within a single program.

Discuss the evolution of programming languages and how they incorporate multiple paradigms.

Programming languages have evolved significantly and this evolution is closely tied to the incorporation of multiple programming paradigms.

Early Days: Procedural Programming

Languages like Fortran and C were primarily procedural, focusing on sequential execution of instructions. However, even these early languages incorporated elements of structured programming, which introduced control flow structures like loops and conditionals, laying the groundwork for more complex paradigms.

Object-Oriented Revolution

The 1980s and 1990s saw the rise of object-oriented programming (OOP) with languages like Smalltalk, C++, and Java. OOP introduced concepts like encapsulation, inheritance, and polymorphism, enabling developers to model real-world entities and relationships more effectively.

The Multi-Paradigm Era

Modern programming languages recognize the strengths of different paradigms and often incorporate elements of multiple approaches. For example:

C++: Supports procedural, object-oriented, and generic programming.

Python: Combines object-oriented, functional, and imperative features.

JavaScript: Primarily known for object-oriented and functional programming, but also supports imperative styles.

Key Trends in Language Evolution

- **Increased expressiveness**: Languages are becoming more concise and readable.
- **Performance optimization**: Focus on improving execution speed and memory usage.
- **Concurrency and parallelism**: Support for concurrent and parallel programming models.
- **Functional programming features**: Incorporating functional concepts for immutability, higher-order functions, and pure functions.
- **Metaprogramming**: Enabling code to manipulate itself at runtime.

How Programming Paradigms Influence Software Design and Architecture?

The choice of programming paradigm significantly impacts the design and architecture of a software system. Let's explore how each paradigm shapes these aspects:

Procedural Programming

- **Design**: Emphasizes algorithmic thinking, with functions as the core building blocks.
- **Architecture**: Often results in monolithic applications with tightly coupled components.

- **Challenges**: Can lead to spaghetti code for complex systems, and difficulty in maintaining large codebases.

Object-Oriented Programming (OOP)

- **Design**: Focuses on modeling real-world entities as objects, with clear responsibilities and relationships.
- **Architecture**: Promotes modularity, encapsulation, and code reusability.
- **Challenges**: Over-engineering can occur, and performance might be impacted in certain scenarios.

Functional Programming

- **Design**: Emphasizes pure functions, immutability, and higher-order functions.
- **Architecture**: Leads to modular, composable, and concurrent systems.
- **Challenges**: Can be challenging to adopt for developers used to imperative styles, and potential performance overhead in some cases.

Declarative Programming

- **Design**: Focuses on describing the desired outcome rather than the steps to achieve it.
- **Architecture**: Often involves data-centric or rule-based systems.
- **Challenges**: Limited control over execution flow, potential performance implications for complex computations.

Logic Programming

- **Design**: Based on knowledge representation and inference.
- **Architecture**: Suitable for expert systems and artificial intelligence applications.
- **Challenges**: Can be less intuitive for developers without a strong logic background.

Key Considerations

- **Problem Domain**: The nature of the problem often dictates the suitable paradigm.
- **Team Expertise**: The skills and experience of the development team influence the choice.
- **Performance Requirements**: Some paradigms might be better suited for performance-critical applications.
- **Maintainability**: Consider long-term maintenance and evolution of the software.

Practical Examples of Programming Paradigms

Procedural Programming:

Problem: Calculating the factorial of a number.

Solution: Using iterative or recursive functions to compute the factorial.

Code Example using C language

```
int factorial(int n) {
  if (n == 0)
    return 1;
```

```
  else
    return n * factorial(n - 1);
}
```

Object-Oriented Programming:

Problem: Modeling a banking system.

Solution: Create classes like Account, Customer, Transaction, with attributes and methods to represent real-world entities.

Code Example using C# language

```
public class Account {
  private double balance;
  public void deposit(double amount) {
    balance += amount;
  }
  public void withdraw(double amount) {
    if (balance >= amount) {
      balance -= amount;
    } else {
      // Handle insufficient funds
    }
  }
}
```

Functional Programming:

Problem: Filtering a list of numbers to find even numbers.

Solution: Using higher-order functions like filter.

Code Example using Python language

```
numbers = [1, 2, 3, 4, 5]

even_numbers = list(filter(lambda x: x % 2 == 0, numbers))
```

Declarative Programming:

Problem: Retrieving data from a database.

Solution: Using SQL to specify the desired data without describing the exact steps.

Code Example using SQL

```
SELECT * FROM Customers WHERE City = 'Delhi';
```

Logic Programming:

Problem: Solving a puzzle like Sudoku.

Solution: Defining rules and constraints, letting the Prolog engine find solutions.

Code Example using Prolog

```
sudoku(Board) :-

   % rules to define valid Sudoku board
```

Explain Object-Oriented Programming (OOP) Concepts.

Object-Oriented Programming (OOP) is a programming paradigm that revolves around the concept of "objects" that contain data (attributes or properties) and code (methods or functions) that operate on that data.

Core Principles of OOP

1. Encapsulation:

- Bundling data and methods that operate on that data within a single unit (class).
- Protecting data from outside interference through access modifiers (public, private, protected).

```
public class Account
{
  private double balance;
  public void Deposit(double amount)
  {
    balance += amount;
  }
  public void Withdraw(double amount)
  {
    if (balance >= amount)
    {
      balance -= amount;
    }
    else
    {
```

```
            Console.WriteLine("Insufficient funds");
        }
    }
}
```

2. Inheritance:

- Creating new classes (derived classes) based on existing classes (base classes).
- Inheriting properties and methods from the base class.
- Extending functionality by adding new members.

```
public class SavingsAccount : Account
{
    public double InterestRate { get; set; }
    public void CalculateInterest()
    {
        // Calculate interest based on balance and interest rate
    }
}
```

3. Polymorphism:

- The ability of objects to take on multiple forms.
- Overloading: Different methods with the same name but different parameters.
- Overriding: Redefining a virtual method in a derived class.

```
public class Shape
```

```
{
  public virtual double Area()
  {
    return 0;
  }
}
public class Circle : Shape
{
  public double Radius { get; set; }
  public override double Area()
  {
    return Math.PI * Radius * Radius;
  }
}
```

4. Abstraction:

- Focusing on essential features while hiding implementation details.
- Using interfaces and abstract classes to define contracts.

```
public interface IShape
{
  double Area();
}
```

Additional OOP Concepts

- **Classes and Objects:** Blueprint for creating objects and instances of that blueprint.
- **Constructors:** Special methods called when an object is created.
- **Destructors:** Clean up resources before an object is destroyed (less common in C# due to garbage collection).
- **Properties:** Provide a controlled way to access and modify object data.

Indexers: Allow array-like access to object members.

CHAPTER 3

.NET HISTORY

A Comprehensive Look at .NET Framework Versions

.NET Framework 1.0 (Released January 15, 2002)

- Introduced managed code execution, Common Language Runtime (CLR), and Base Class Library (BCL).
- Laid the foundation for language interoperability (C#, VB.NET, etc.).
- Introduced ASP.NET for web development.
- Windows Forms for desktop applications.
- ADO.NET for data access.

.NET Framework 1.1 (Released April 13, 2003)

- Improved performance and stability.
- Added support for mobile devices.
- Enhanced ASP.NET with new controls and features.
- Introduced new classes for security and configuration.

.NET Framework 2.0 (Released November 22, 2005)

- Significant performance improvements.
- Introduced Generics for type safety and performance.
- Enhanced data access with LINQ to DataSet.
- Added new controls for Windows Forms and ASP.NET.
- Introduced partial classes and anonymous methods.

.NET Framework 3.0 (Released November 6, 2006)

- Not a full framework version but an extension to .NET 2.0.
- Introduced Windows Presentation Foundation (WPF) for rich user interfaces.
- Added Windows Communication Foundation (WCF) for service-oriented architecture.
- Included Windows Workflow Foundation (WF) for workflow-based applications.
- Introduced Windows CardSpace for identity management.

.NET Framework 3.5 (Released November 19, 2007)

- Built on .NET 2.0 and 3.0.
- Added LINQ to Objects, LINQ to XML, and LINQ to SQL.
- Enhanced ASP.NET AJAX for rich internet applications.
- Improved performance and reliability.

.NET Framework 4.0 (Released April 20, 2010)

- Major overhaul with new CLR version (4.0).

- Introduced Parallel Computing for multi-core processors.
- Enhanced dynamic language runtime (DLR).
- Improved WPF and WCF with new features.
- Added support for IronPython and IronRuby.

.NET Framework 4.5 (Released August 15, 2012, End of Life: January 12, 2016)

- Async/Await for asynchronous programming.
- Improved garbage collection.
- Enhanced ASP.NET with MVC 5 and Web API.
- Added support for Windows Store apps.

.NET Framework 4.6 (Released July 20, 2015, End of Life: Retired on April 26, 2022, due to SHA-1 certificate issues.)

- Improved performance and reliability.
- Enhanced ASP.NET with HTTP/2 support.
- Added support for new hardware features.
- Improved debugging and diagnostics.

.NET Framework 4.7 (Released April 5, 2017)

- High DPI support for better scaling on high-resolution displays.
- Improved performance and reliability.
- Enhanced cryptography support.

- Added support for new Windows features.

.NET Framework 4.8 (Released April 18, 2019)

- Last major release of the .NET Framework.
- Improved reliability and performance.
- Added support for new Windows features.
- Enhanced compatibility with older applications.

Note: Microsoft has shifted its focus to .NET Core (now .NET) as the primary development platform. While .NET Framework continues to be supported, new features and investments are primarily directed towards .NET.

A Comprehensive Look at C# Versions

C# has evolved significantly since its inception, incorporating new features and paradigms to meet the evolving needs of developers. Let's delve into the key changes introduced with each version:

C# 1.0 (2000)

- The foundational version, introducing core object-oriented constructs: classes, structs, interfaces, inheritance, polymorphism, and properties.
- Emphasis on managed code execution and integration with the .NET Framework.

C# 2.0 (2005)

- **Generics:** Introduced to improve type safety and performance.
- **Partial classes:** Enabling code splitting across multiple files.
- **Iterators:** Simplified collection iteration.

- **Anonymous methods:** Facilitated delegate creation without explicit method declaration.
- **Nullable types:** Allowed for optional value types.

C# 3.0 (2007)

- **Language Integrated Query (LINQ):** Powerful query syntax for various data sources.
- **Lambda expressions:** Concise syntax for anonymous functions.
- **Extension methods:** Extending existing types without modifying them.
- **Implicitly typed local variables:** var keyword for automatic type inference.
- **Object and collection initializers:** Simplified object creation.

C# 4.0 (2010)

- **Dynamic typing:** Interoperability with dynamic languages.
- **Named and optional parameters:** Increased flexibility in method calls.
- **COM interop improvements:** Enhanced interaction with COM components.
- **Generic covariance and contravariance:** Improved type safety and flexibility.

C# 5.0 (2012)

- **Async/await:** Simplified asynchronous programming.

C# 6.0 (2015)

- **Expression-bodied members:** Concise syntax for methods, properties, and constructors.
- **Null-conditional operator:** Safe null handling.
- **String interpolation:** Enhanced string formatting.
- **Auto-property initializers:** Simplified property initialization.
- **Exception filters:** More granular exception handling.

C# 7.0 (2017)

- **Tuples:** Immutable value types for grouping data.
- **Pattern matching:** Improved type checking and conditional logic.
- **Local functions:** Nested functions within methods.
- **Ref locals and returns:** Improved performance in certain scenarios.
- **Out variables:** Simplified method arguments.

C# 8.0 (2019)

- **Nullable reference types:** Improved null safety.
- **Asynchronous streams:** Efficiently process asynchronous sequences.
- **Default interface methods:** Added default implementations to interfaces.
- **Pattern matching enhancements:** Expanded pattern matching capabilities.

- **Switch expressions:** Simplified switch statements.

C# 9.0 (2020)

- **Top-level statements:** Omitted Main method for simple programs.
- **Records:** Immutable data structures.
- **Init-only setters:** Restricted property modification after object creation.
- **Pattern matching improvements:** Enhanced pattern matching capabilities.
- **Covariant returns:** Allowed derived methods to return more specific types.

C# 10 (2022)

- **File-scoped namespaces:** Simplified namespace declarations.
- **Interpolated string handlers:** Custom formatting for interpolated strings.
- **Record structs:** Value-type records.
- **Structure types:** Improved performance and memory usage.
- **Extended property patterns:** Enhanced pattern matching with property access.

C# 11 (2022)

- **Raw string literals:** Simplified handling of multi-line strings.
- **Generic math:** Improved performance for generic math operations.
- **List patterns:** Enhanced pattern matching for lists.

- **Required members:** Guaranteed initialization of properties.

C# 12

- **Primary Constructors**: This feature allows for a more concise and expressive way to define constructors, improving code readability.
- **Collection Expressions**: A new syntax for creating collections, providing a more fluent and expressive way to initialize collections.
- **Inline Arrays**: The ability to create arrays directly within a struct, enhancing performance and type safety.
- **Optional Parameters in Lambda Expressions**: Similar to method parameters, lambda expressions can now have optional parameters.
- **Ref readonly Parameters**: Improve clarity and safety when using ref parameters.
- **Alias any type**: Allows creating aliases for any type, not just named types.
- **Experimental attribute**: Indicates experimental features that might change in future versions.
- **Interceptors**: A preview feature for intercepting method calls.

Chapter 4

.NET Framework

What is .NET Framework?

The .NET Framework is a software development framework developed by Microsoft that runs primarily on the Windows operating system. It provides a runtime environment and a rich set of classes for building various types of applications, including desktop, web, and mobile applications.

Benefits of Using .NET Framework:

- **Rapid development**: Provides a rich set of classes and tools to accelerate development.
- **Language interoperability**: Ability to use different languages within the same application.
- **Security**: Built-in security features protect applications from vulnerabilities.
- **Memory management**: Automatic garbage collection simplifies memory management.
- **Deployment**: Easy deployment of applications.

Limitations of .NET Framework:

- **Windows-centric**: Primarily designed for Windows platforms.
- **Performance overhead**: Compared to native code, .NET applications might have slightly lower performance.

While .NET Framework has been a cornerstone for Windows development, Microsoft has introduced .NET Core (now .NET) as a cross-platform successor with improved performance and flexibility.

Explain each component of the .NET Framework.

The .NET Framework is composed of several key components that work together to provide a robust platform for application development.

1. Common Language Runtime (CLR)

- The execution engine for .NET applications.
- Manages memory allocation, thread management, garbage collection, and code safety.
- Provides services like exception handling, type checking, and security.
- Ensures language interoperability, allowing different .NET languages to interact seamlessly.

2. .NET Framework Class Library (FCL)

- A vast collection of reusable classes, interfaces, and value types.
- Offers pre-built functionality for common tasks like input/output, string manipulation, data structures, networking, and more.
- Provides a foundation for building applications in various

domains.

3. Common Type System (CTS)

- Defines a common type system for all .NET languages.
- Ensures type safety and compatibility between different languages.
- Specifies rules for data types, their representation, and operations.

4. ASP.NET

- A framework for building web applications and services.
- Provides a platform for creating dynamic web pages, web services, and web APIs.
- Supports different development models like Web Forms, MVC, and Web API.

5. Windows Forms

- A graphical user interface (GUI) framework for building desktop applications.
- Provides a set of controls for creating forms, menus, and other UI elements.

6. ADO.NET

- A data access technology for interacting with databases.
- Offers a disconnected data model for efficient data handling.
- Supports various data sources like SQL Server, Oracle, and others.

7. Language Integration

- Supports multiple languages like C#, VB.NET, F#, and others.
- Enables code interoperability and sharing between different languages.

8. Common Language Specification (CLS)

- Defines a set of rules and conventions for .NET languages.
- Ensures compatibility and interoperability between different languages.

These are the core components of the .NET Framework, providing a comprehensive platform for building applications. Each component plays a crucial role in the development and execution of .NET applications.

Explain how these .NET Framework components interact with each other.

The .NET Framework components work in concert to provide a comprehensive development platform. Let's understand this in detail:

CLR as the Foundation

- **Execution Environment**: The CLR serves as the runtime environment for .NET applications, managing memory, threads, and code execution.
- **Language Interoperability**: Different .NET languages compile into Common Intermediate Language (CIL), allowing seamless interaction between code written in different languages.
- **Base Class Library (BCL)**: The CLR provides access to the BCL, offering a rich set of classes for various functionalities.

FCL and CTS: Building Blocks:

- **Common Type System (CTS)**: Defines the rules for data types and their operations, ensuring type safety and compatibility across languages.
- **Framework Class Library (FCL)**: Leverages the CTS to provide a vast collection of reusable classes, forming the backbone of .NET applications.
- **Language Integration**: .NET languages like C#, VB.NET, and F# utilize the CTS and FCL to interact with the CLR.

ASP.NET and Windows Forms: Leveraging the Framework

- **UI Frameworks**: ASP.NET and Windows Forms build upon the CLR and FCL to provide UI development capabilities.
- **Data Access**: Both frameworks rely on ADO.NET to interact with databases.
- **Language Integration**: Developers can use any .NET language to build applications using these frameworks.

Data Access with ADO.NET

- **CLR and CTS**: ADO.NET is built on top of the CLR and adheres to the CTS for type safety.
- **FCL**: Provides base classes for data access functionality.
- **Data Providers**: Specific data providers (e.g., SqlClient, OleDb) interact with databases.

In essence, the CLR acts as the foundation, providing the execution environment and core services. The FCL offers a rich set of classes for developers to build upon. Languages like C# and VB.NET leverage the CLR and FCL to create applications. UI frameworks like ASP.NET and Windows Forms utilize the underlying infrastructure to provide UI capabilities, while ADO.NET handles data access.

Explain memory management in .NET Framework.

The .NET Framework employs a **garbage collector (GC)** to automate memory management, relieving developers from the burden of manual memory allocation and deallocation. This significantly reduces the risk of memory leaks and improves application reliability.

The Managed Heap

When a .NET application starts, a region of memory is allocated called the **managed heap**. This is where objects are stored. The GC is responsible for tracking object usage and reclaiming memory when objects are no longer needed.

Garbage Collection Process

The GC operates in generations to optimize performance:

- **Generation 0:** Newly created objects reside here.
- **Generation 1:** Objects that survive a Generation 0 collection are promoted to Generation 1.
- **Generation 2:** Objects that survive multiple collections are moved to Generation 2.

The GC periodically scans the heap, identifying no longer referenced objects. These objects are marked for collection and their memory is reclaimed.

Key Points

- **Automatic memory management:** Developers don't need to deallocate memory manually.
- **Generational garbage collection:** Improves performance by

focusing on short-lived objects.

- **Deterministic finalization:** Allows for custom cleanup code using the Finalize method, but use it cautiously.

Additional Considerations

- **Large Object Heap (LOH):** Objects larger than a certain threshold are placed on the LOH, which has different collection behavior.
- **Memory Leaks:** While the GC is powerful, it's still possible to introduce memory leaks if objects are held onto unnecessarily.
- **Performance Impact:** Excessive garbage collection can impact performance. Proper object management and design can help mitigate this.

Developers can write more efficient and reliable code by understanding how the .NET garbage collector works.

What is GC.Collect() function? How it impacts the memory management?

GC.Collect() is a method in the .NET Framework that forces the garbage collector to run immediately. Normally, the garbage collector operates automatically, reclaiming memory for objects that are no longer referenced. However, there are specific scenarios where you might consider using GC.Collect():

- **Debugging memory-related issues:** To force a collection and inspect memory usage.
- **Very specific performance optimization:** In rare cases, where precise control over memory is crucial and the performance impact is carefully considered.

Important Considerations:

- **Performance impact:** Calling GC.Collect() can negatively impact application performance.

- **Unpredictable behavior:** The exact behavior of GC.Collect() can vary depending on the system and the garbage collector's internal state.
- **Managed by the runtime:** The garbage collector is generally more efficient at managing memory than manual intervention.

Generally, it's recommended to avoid using GC.Collect() unless absolutely necessary.

Best practices for memory management include:

- Understanding object lifetimes.
- Minimizing object creation.
- Using IDisposable for unmanaged resources.
- Profiling memory usage to identify potential issues.

By following these guidelines, you can achieve better performance and reliability without relying on explicit garbage collection calls.

How we can use IDisposable for unmanaged resources?

IDisposable is an interface in .NET that provides a mechanism for releasing unmanaged resources explicitly. Unmanaged resources are those that aren't managed by the garbage collector, such as file handles, database connections, network sockets, and graphics handles.

Implementing IDisposable

To implement IDisposable, a class must:

1. **Implement the IDisposable interface:** This indicates that the class contains unmanaged resources.
2. **Override the Dispose method:** This method performs the

cleanup of unmanaged resources.

```
public class MyResource : IDisposable {
private bool disposedValue = false; // Todetect redundant calls
protected virtual void Dispose(bool disposing)
{
  if(!disposedValue)
  {
    if (disposing)
    {
      // Dispose managed resources
      // e.g., close managed objects
    }
    // Dispose unmanaged resources (unmanaged code only)
    // e.g., close file handles, database connections
     disposedValue = true;
  }
}
public void Dispose()
{
  Dispose(true);
  GC.SuppressFinalize(this);
}
}
```

Using IDisposable

To use an IDisposable object, you should use a using statement:

using (MyResource resource = new MyResource()) { // Use the resource
}

The using statement ensures that the Dispose method is called even if an exception occurs.

Important Considerations

- **Dispose Pattern:** The provided code demonstrates the correct way to implement Dispose to handle both managed and unmanaged resources.
- **Finalizer:** The Finalize method is used for final cleanup but should be avoided if possible.
- **Deterministic Release:** Using IDisposable ensures timely release of unmanaged resources.
- **Null Checks:** Always check for null before calling Dispose to prevent exceptions.

What are the potential pitfalls when using IDisposable?

While IDisposable is a powerful tool for managing unmanaged resources, it's essential to be aware of potential pitfalls to avoid issues.

1. Incorrect Implementation of Dispose Pattern:

- **Missing Dispose(bool disposing) overload:** This is crucial for handling both managed and unmanaged resources correctly.
- **Incorrect resource disposal:** Ensure that all unmanaged resources are released in the Dispose(bool disposing) method.

- **Redundant calls to Dispose:** Calling Dispose multiple times can lead to exceptions.

2. Misuse of the using Statement:

- **Nested using statements:** While technically possible, it can lead to unexpected behavior if the inner using block disposes of resources used by the outer block.
- **Exceptions:** If an exception occurs before the end of the using block, the resource might not be disposed of correctly. Consider using a try-finally block for additional safety.

3. Ignoring Finalizers:

- While Finalize can be used for cleanup, it's generally discouraged due to performance implications and potential issues.
- If you must use a finalizer, ensure it's kept simple and avoids resource-intensive operations.

4. Resource Leaks:

- **Forgotten Dispose calls:** Failing to call Dispose explicitly can lead to resource leaks.
- **Incorrect handling of exceptions:** Exceptions can prevent Dispose from being called.
- **Object lifetime management:** Ensure objects are disposed of when no longer needed.

5. Performance Considerations:

- **Excessive Dispose calls:** Calling Dispose too frequently can impact performance.
- **Object pooling:** Consider object pooling for frequently used

resources.

What are Managed and Unmanaged code in the .NET Framework?

Managed Code

- Runs under the control of the Common Language Runtime (CLR).
- Benefits from automatic memory management, garbage collection, and type safety.
- Compiles to intermediate language (IL) which is then executed by the CLR.
- Examples: C#, VB.NET, F#
- Security: Enhanced security due to CLR's runtime checks and protections.

Unmanaged Code

- Runs directly on the hardware without the supervision of a runtime environment.
- Requires manual memory management, error handling, and security considerations.
- Compiles directly to machine code.
- Examples: C++, assembly language
- Performance: Generally offers better performance due to direct hardware interaction but demands more expertise.

Types of Assemblies in .NET

An assembly is the fundamental building block of .NET applications. It's a collection of types (classes, interfaces, enums, etc.) and resources that form a logical unit of functionality.

Types of Assemblies

1. **Private Assemblies:**
   - Used exclusively by a single application.
   - Typically located in the application's directory or subdirectories.
   - No registration required.
2. **Shared Assemblies:**
   - Can be shared by multiple applications.
   - Stored in the Global Assembly Cache (GAC).
   - Requires strong naming (signing with a strong name key).
3. **Satellite Assemblies:**
   - Contain localized resources for an application (e.g., culture-specific text, images).
   - Dependent on a main assembly.

Additional Notes

- **Dynamic Assemblies:** Created in memory at runtime and not saved to disk.
- **Process Assemblies (EXE):** Define the entry point of an application.
- **Library Assemblies (DLL):** Contain reusable code for

multiple applications.

Key Components of an Assembly

- **Manifest:** Contains metadata about the assembly, including version, culture, strong name, dependencies, and exported types.
- **Type Metadata:** Describes the types defined in the assembly.
- **Intermediate Language (IL):** The compiled code that is executed by the CLR.
- **Resources:** Additional data like images, strings, and other assets.

What are Shared Assemblies and how to create shared assemblies?

Shared Assemblies (Strong-Named Assemblies):

- Can be shared by multiple applications.
- Require a strong name (public key, assembly name, version, culture, and token).
- Deployed to the Global Assembly Cache (GAC) or side-by-side.

Steps to Create a Strong-Named Assembly

1. **Generate a Strong Name Key:** Use the sn.exe tool to create a key file.
2. **Sign the Assembly:** Use the /keyfile option during compilation to sign the assembly with the strong name key.
3. **Deploy to GAC:** Use the gacutil.exe tool to install the assembly in the GAC.

What is MSIL or Microsoft Intermediate Language?

MSIL, also known as CIL (Common Intermediate Language), is an assembly-like language that serves as an intermediate representation of managed code. It's generated by .NET compilers from source code written in languages like C#, VB.NET, or F#.

Key characteristics of MSIL:

- Platform-independent: It can be executed on any platform with a .NET runtime.
- Object-oriented: Supports object-oriented concepts like classes, interfaces, and inheritance.
- Managed code: Benefits from the CLR's garbage collection and type safety.
- Verifiable: Can be statically verified for type safety and security.

What is JIT or JIT (Just-In-Time) Compiler?

The JIT compiler is a component of the CLR that translates MSIL code into native machine code at runtime. This process is called compilation.

Key features of JIT:

- **Dynamic compilation:** Only compiles the necessary code when it's first executed.
- **Optimization:** Can apply various optimization techniques to improve performance.
- **Caching:** Stores compiled code for future use.
- **Platform-specific code generation:** Produces machine code tailored to the specific CPU architecture.

Benefits of JIT compilation:

- **Improved performance:** By compiling code at runtime, the JIT compiler can optimize it based on the specific hardware and software environment.
- **Cross-platform compatibility:** MSIL code can be executed on different platforms by using platform-specific JIT compilers.
- **Faster startup:** Only the necessary code is compiled, reducing startup time.

What is the .NET Framework Class Library (FCL)?

The .NET Framework Class Library (FCL) is a collection of reusable types (classes, interfaces, and value types) that provide access to system functionality. It's a core component of the .NET Framework, offering a vast array of pre-built functionality for developers to leverage in their applications.

Key Features of FCL

- **Base data types:** Provides fundamental data types like integers, floating-point numbers, characters, and booleans.
- **Input/output operations:** Offers classes for file and stream operations.
- **String manipulation:** Provides classes for working with strings, including searching, formatting, and parsing.
- **Collections:** Offers various collection types (arrays, lists, dictionaries, etc.) for data management.
- **Networking:** Supports network communication, including TCP/IP, HTTP, FTP, and more.
- **Security:** Provides classes for cryptography, authentication, and authorization.

- **XML support:** Offers classes for working with XML documents.
- **Reflection:** Allows runtime inspection of types and assemblies.
- **Serialization:** Enables object serialization and deserialization.
- **Threading:** Provides classes for multi-threaded programming.
- **Windows Forms and ASP.NET:** Includes classes for building user interfaces.

Importance of FCL

- **Accelerates development:** By providing pre-built functionality, FCL significantly reduces development time.
- **Consistent API:** Offers a unified programming model across different application types.
- **Quality and reliability:** FCL is extensively tested and optimized.
- **Cross-language compatibility:** Can be used with different .NET languages.

Essentially, the FCL acts as a foundation for building applications on the .NET platform, offering a rich set of tools and utilities to developers.

CHAPTER 5

DESIGN PATTERNS

What are the design patterns in C#?

Design patterns are reusable solutions to common software design problems. They provide a proven template for solving specific issues, and improving code quality, maintainability, and reusability. Here are some of the most commonly used design patterns in C#:

Creational Patterns

- **Singleton:** Ensures that a class has only one instance and provides a global point of access to it.
- **Factory:** Creates objects without exposing the instantiation logic.
- **Abstract Factory:** Provides an interface for creating families of related or dependent objects without specifying their concrete classes.
- **Builder:** Separates the construction of a complex object from its representation, allowing you to create different representations of the same object.
- **Prototype:** Creates new objects by copying existing objects.

Structural Patterns

- **Adapter:** Converts the interface of a class into another interface that clients expect.
- **Bridge:** Decouples an abstraction from its implementation, allowing them to vary independently.
- **Composite:** Composes objects into tree structures to represent part-whole hierarchies.
- **Decorator:** Attaches additional responsibilities to an object dynamically.
- **Facade:** Provides a unified interface to a set of interfaces in a subsystem.
- **Flyweight:** Reduces the number of objects by sharing common data.
- **Proxy:** Provides a surrogate or placeholder for another object to control access to it.

Behavioral Patterns

- **Strategy:** Defines a family of algorithms, encapsulates each one, and makes them interchangeable.
- **Observer:** Defines a one-to-many dependency between objects so that when one object changes state, all its dependents are notified and updated automatically.
- **Iterator:** Provides a way to access the elements of an aggregate object sequentially without exposing its underlying representation.
- **Template Method:** Defines the skeleton of an algorithm in an operation, deferring some steps to subclasses.
- **Command:** Encapsulates a request as an object, thereby letting you parameterize clients with different requests, queue or log

requests, and support undoable operations.

- **State:** Allows an object to alter its behavior when its internal state changes.
- **Visitor:** Represents an operation to be performed on the elements of an object structure.
- **Mediator:** Defines an object that encapsulates how a set of objects interact.
- **Memento:** Captures and externalizes an object's internal state so that it can be restored to this state later.

Choosing the Right Design Pattern: The best design pattern for a given problem depends on the specific requirements and constraints. Consider factors such as:

- **Complexity of the problem**
- **Maintainability**
- **Performance**
- **Reusability**

By understanding and applying these design patterns, you can write more maintainable, scalable, and efficient C# code.

Explain the Singleton Pattern in C#?

The Singleton pattern is a creational design pattern that ensures a class has only one instance and provides a global point of access to it. This is useful for situations where you need to control the creation of objects and ensure that there is only one instance of a particular class.

Key Characteristics:

- **Single Instance:** Only one instance of the class can be created.
- **Global Access:** The class provides a static method to access the single instance.

- **Thread Safety:** The implementation must be thread-safe to prevent multiple instances from being created simultaneously.

Advantages:

- **Controlled Creation:** Ensures only one instance of the class exists.
- **Global Access:** Provides a convenient way to access the instance from anywhere in the application.
- **Performance:** Can be optimized for performance by caching the instance.

Disadvantages:

- **Global State:** Can introduce global state, which can make code harder to test and maintain.
- **Tight Coupling:** Can create tight coupling between different parts of the application.

When to Use:

- When you need to control the creation of objects and ensure that there is only one instance.
- When you need to provide a global point of access to a shared resource.
- When you want to avoid creating multiple instances of a resource-intensive object.

Important Considerations:

- **Thread Safety:** Ensure that the implementation is thread-safe to prevent multiple instances from being created simultaneously.
- **Global State:** Be mindful of the potential downsides of global state and consider alternative approaches if necessary.
- **Alternative Patterns:** Explore alternative patterns like

Dependency Injection or Service Locator if the Singleton pattern doesn't fit your needs.

Explain all the ways in which a singleton class can be created in C#?

1. No Thread Safety

```
public sealed class Singleton
{
  private static Singleton instance = null;
  private Singleton()
   {
   }
  public static Singleton Instance
   {
     get
     {
       if (instance == null)
       {
         instance = new Singleton();
       }
       return instance;
     }
   }
}
```

2. Thread Safety

```
public sealed class Singleton
{
  private static Singleton instance = null;
  private static readonly object lockobj = new object();
  Singleton()
   {
   }
  public static Singleton Instance
   {
     get
     {
        lock (lockobj)
        {
           if (instance == null)
           {
              instance = new Singleton();
           }
           return instance;
        }
     }
   }
```

```
}
```

3. Double-Check Locking

```
public sealed class Singleton
{
  private static Singleton instance = null;
  private static readonly object lockobj = new object();
  Singleton()
  {
  }
  public static Singleton Instance
  {
    get
    {
      if (instance == null)
      {
        lock (lockobj)
        {
          if (instance == null)
          {
            instance = newSingleton();
          }
        }
```

```
        }
        return instance;
      }
    }
}
```

4. Eager Instantiation, without Locking

```
public sealed class Singleton
{
  private static readonly Singleton instance = new Singleton();
  //Explicit static constructor to tell C# compiler
  static Singleton()  {   }
  private Singleton()  {  }
  public static Singleton Instance
  {
    get
    {
      return instance;
    }
  }
}
```

5. Lazy Instantiation

```
public sealed class Singleton
```

```
{
  private Singleton()  { }
  public static Singleton Instance { get { return Nested.instance; } }
  private class Nested
   {
     // Explicit static constructor to tell C# compiler
     static Nested()     {     }
     internal static readonly Singleton instance = new Singleton();
   }
}
```

6. using Lazy<T> type

```
public sealed class Singleton
{
  private static readonly Lazy<Singleton> lazy =
     new Lazy<Singleton>(() => new Singleton());
  public static Singleton Instance { get { return lazy.Value; } }
  private Singleton()  { }
}
```

Explain Factory Pattern in C#.

The Factory Pattern is a creational design pattern that provides a way to create objects without exposing the instantiation logic. It encapsulates the object creation process, making the code more flexible and easier to maintain.

Key Components:

- **Factory Interface:** Defines a method for creating objects.
- **Concrete Factories:** Implement the factory interface and provide specific implementations for creating objects.
- **Products:** The objects that are created by the factories.

Benefits of the Factory Pattern:

- **Decoupling:** Separates the creation of objects from their usage.
- **Flexibility:** Allows for easy changes to the creation process without affecting client code.
- **Extensibility:** New object types can be added without modifying existing code.
- **Testing:** Makes it easier to test different implementations of the factory.

Example of Factory Pattern in C#.

```
interface IShape

{

  voidDraw();

}

class Circle : IShape

{

  public void Draw() => Console.WriteLine("Drawing acircle");

}

class Rectangle : IShape
```

```
{
   publicvoid Draw() => Console.WriteLine("Drawing a rectangle");
}
interface IShapeFactory
{
  IShape CreateShape();
}
class ShapeFactory : IShapeFactory
{
  public IShape CreateShape(string shapeType)
  {
    switch (shapeType)
    {
        case "circle":
          return new Circle();
        case "rectangle":
          return new Rectangle();
        default:
          throw new ArgumentException("Invalid shape type");
    }
  }
}
class Program
```

```
{
  static void Main()
  {
    IShapeFactory factory = new ShapeFactory();
    IShape circle = factory.CreateShape("circle");
    IShape rectangle = factory.CreateShape("rectangle");
    circle.Draw();
    rectangle.Draw();
  }
}
```

In this example:

- IShape is the interface defining the Draw method.
- Circle and Rectangle are concrete implementations of the IShape interface.
- IShapeFactory is the factory interface.
- ShapeFactory is the concrete factory that creates instances of Circle and Rectangle based on the provided shape type.

The ShapeFactory class encapsulates the object creation logic, making it easier to change the implementation of the factory without affecting the client code. This promotes flexibility and maintainability.

Explain Abstract Factory pattern in C#.

The Abstract Factory Pattern is a creational design pattern that provides an interface for creating families of related or dependent objects without specifying their concrete classes. It allows you to create different product families without coupling the client code to concrete classes.

Key Components:

- **Abstract Factory:** Defines an interface for creating families of related or dependent objects.
- **Concrete Factories:** Implement the abstract factory interface and provide specific implementations for creating objects.
- **Abstract Products:** Define interfaces for the products.
- **Concrete Products:** Implement the abstract product interfaces and represent the actual products.

Example of Abstract Factory Pattern in C#.

```
interface IShape

{

  voidDraw();

}

class Circle : IShape

{

  public void Draw() => Console.WriteLine("Drawing acircle");

}

class Rectangle : IShape

{

  public void Draw() => Console.WriteLine("Drawing a rectangle");

}

interface IColor

{
```

```
    voidFill();
}
class Red : IColor
{
    public void Fill() => Console.WriteLine("Filling with red");
}
class Blue : IColor
{
    public void Fill() => Console.WriteLine("Filling with blue");
}
interface IShapeFactory
{
    IShape CreateShape();
    IColor CreateColor();
}
class ShapeFactory1 : IShapeFactory
{
    public IShape CreateShape() => new Circle();
    public IColor CreateColor() => new Red();
}
class ShapeFactory2 : IShapeFactory
{
    public IShape CreateShape() => new Rectangle();
```

```
  public IColor CreateColor() => new Blue();
}
class Program
{
  static void Main()
  {
    IShapeFactory factory1 = new ShapeFactory1();
    IShape shape1 = factory1.CreateShape();
    IColor color1 = factory1.CreateColor();
    shape1.Draw();
    color1.Fill();
    IShapeFactory factory2 = new ShapeFactory2();
    IShape shape2 = factory2.CreateShape();
    IColor color2 = factory2.CreateColor();
    shape2.Draw();
    color2.Fill();
  }
}
```

In this example:

- IShape and IColor are the abstract product interfaces.
- Circle, Rectangle, Red, and Blue are the concrete product classes.
- IShapeFactory is the abstract factory interface.

- ShapeFactory1 and ShapeFactory2 are the concrete factory classes that create different combinations of shapes and colors.

Explain Builder design pattern in C#.

The Builder pattern is a creational design pattern that separates the construction of a complex object from its representation. It allows you to create different representations of the same object using the same construction process.

Key Components:

- **Director:** Coordinates the construction process and calls the builder methods.
- **Builder:** Defines an abstract interface for constructing parts of the product.
- **Concrete Builders:** Implement the builder interface and provide specific implementations for constructing parts of the product.
- **Product:** Represents the final product that is constructed by the builder.

The Builder pattern allows you to create different configurations of the same product without tightly coupling the client code to the construction process. This makes it easier to extend and modify the product without affecting existing code.

Example of Builder Pattern in C#.

```
interface IComputerBuilder

{

  voidBuildCPU();

  voidBuildRAM();
```

```
voidBuildHDD();
Computer GetComputer();
}
class Computer
{
public string CPU { get; set; }
public int RAM { get; set; }
public int HDD { get; set; }
}
class CheapComputerBuilder : IComputerBuilder
{
private Computer computer = new Computer();
public void BuildCPU() => computer.CPU = "Intel Celeron";
public void BuildRAM() => computer.RAM = 4;
public void BuildHDD() => computer.HDD = 500;
public Computer GetComputer() => computer;
}
class ExpensiveComputerBuilder :IComputerBuilder
{
private Computer computer = new Computer();
public void BuildCPU() => computer.CPU = "Intel Core i7";
publicvoid BuildRAM() => computer.RAM = 16;
public void BuildHDD() => computer.HDD = 1000;
```

```
  public Computer GetComputer() => computer;
}


class ComputerDirector
{
  public Computer BuildComputer(IComputerBuilder builder)
  {
    builder.BuildCPU();
    builder.BuildRAM();
    builder.BuildHDD();
    return builder.GetComputer();
  }
}
class Program
{
  static void Main()
  {
    ComputerDirector director = new ComputerDirector();
    IComputerBuilder cheapBuilder = new
CheapComputerBuilder();
    IComputerBuilder expensiveBuilder = new
ExpensiveComputerBuilder();
    Computer cheapComputer =
director.BuildComputer(cheapBuilder);
```

```
        Computer expensiveComputer = director.BuildComputer(expensiveBuilder);

        Console.WriteLine(cheapComputer.CPU);

        Console.WriteLine(cheapComputer.RAM);

        Console.WriteLine(cheapComputer.HDD);

        Console.WriteLine(expensiveComputer.CPU);

        Console.WriteLine(expensiveComputer.RAM);

        Console.WriteLine(expensiveComputer.HDD);

    }

}
```

In this example:

- IComputerBuilder is the builder interface.
- CheapComputerBuilder and ExpensiveComputerBuilder are concrete builders that implement the builder interface.
- Computer is the product class.
- ComputerDirector coordinates the construction process by calling the builder methods.

Explain Prototype design pattern in C#.

The Prototype pattern is a creational design pattern that provides a way to create new objects by copying existing objects. This can be useful when you need to create many similar objects without having to re-create them from scratch.

Key Components:

- **Prototype:** Defines an interface for creating a new object.

- **Concrete Prototype:** Implements the prototype interface and provides a method for cloning itself.
- **Client:** Creates new objects by cloning existing prototypes.

The Prototype pattern can be useful when you need to create many similar objects efficiently, especially when the objects are complex or expensive to create. It can also be used to implement object pooling or caching.

Example of Prototype Pattern in C#.

```
interface IShape
{
  IShape Clone();
  voidDraw();
}
class Circle : IShape
{
  public int Radius { get; set; }
  public Circle(int radius)
  {
    Radius = radius;
  }
  public IShape Clone() => new Circle(Radius);
  public void Draw() => Console.WriteLine("Drawing a circle with radius: " + Radius);
}
class Rectangle : IShape
```

```
{
  public int Width { get; set; }
  public int Height { get; set; }
  public Rectangle(int width, int height)
  {
    Width = width;
    Height = height;
  }
  public IShape Clone() => newRectangle(Width, Height);
  public void Draw() => Console.WriteLine("Drawing a rectangle with width: " + Width + " and height: " + Height);
}
class Program
{
  static void Main()
  {
    IShape circle = new Circle(5);
    IShape clonedCircle = circle.Clone();
    circle.Draw();
    clonedCircle.Draw();
    IShape rectangle = new Rectangle(10, 20);
    IShape clonedRectangle = rectangle.Clone();
    rectangle.Draw();
```

```
        clonedRectangle.Draw();
    }
}
```

In this example:

- IShape is the prototype interface that defines a Clone method.
- Circle and Rectangle are concrete prototypes that implement the IShape interface and provide their own cloning logic.
- The Clone method in each class creates a new instance of the same type and copies the relevant properties.

Explain Adapter design pattern in C#.

The Adapter pattern is a structural design pattern that allows incompatible interfaces to work together. It provides a wrapper around an existing interface to adapt it to a new interface that clients expect.

Key Components:

- **Target:** Defines the specific interface that clients expect.
- **Adaptee:** Defines the existing interface that needs to be adapted.
- **Adapter:** Adapts the adaptee interface to the target interface.

Benefits of the Adapter Pattern:

- **Compatibility:** Allows incompatible interfaces to work together.
- **Reusability:** Enables the reuse of existing code without modifying it.
- **Flexibility:** Provides a flexible way to adapt objects to different

interfaces.

The Adapter pattern is a useful design pattern for integrating legacy code with new systems or for adapting third-party libraries to your application's requirements.

Example of Adapter Pattern in C#.

```
interface IShape
{
  voidDraw();
}
class LegacyShape
{
  public void LegacyDraw()
  {
    Console.WriteLine("Drawing a legacy shape");
  }
}
class ShapeAdapter : IShape
{
  private LegacyShape legacyShape;
  public ShapeAdapter(LegacyShape legacyShape)
  {
    this.legacyShape = legacyShape;
  }
```

```
    public void Draw()
    {
        legacyShape.LegacyDraw();
    }
}
class Program
{
    static void Main()
    {
        LegacyShape legacyShape = new LegacyShape();
        IShape shape = new ShapeAdapter(legacyShape);
        shape.Draw();
    }
}
```

In this example:

- IShape is the target interface that clients expect.
- LegacyShape is the adaptee interface that needs to be adapted.
- ShapeAdapter is the adapter that adapts the LegacyShape interface to the IShape interface.

The ShapeAdapter class wraps the LegacyShape object and provides a method Draw that implements the IShape interface. This allows clients to use the LegacyShape object without knowing its specific interface.

Explain Bridge design pattern in C#.

The Bridge pattern is a structural design pattern that decouples an abstraction from its implementation, allowing them to vary independently. This makes it easier to change the implementation of a system without affecting the abstraction.

Key Components:

- **Abstraction:** Defines the high-level interface for the system.
- **Refined Abstraction:** Extends the abstraction and provides specific implementations.
- **Implementor:** Defines the interface for the low-level implementation.
- **Concrete Implementor:** Provides specific implementations of the implementor interface.

Benefits of the Bridge Pattern:

- **Decoupling:** Separates the abstraction from the implementation, making the code more flexible.
- **Reusability:** Allows you to reuse the same abstraction with different implementations.
- **Extensibility:** Makes it easier to add new implementations without affecting existing code.

The Bridge pattern is a useful design pattern for situations where you need to decouple the abstraction from the implementation to improve flexibility and maintainability.

Example of Bridge Pattern in C#.

```
interface IShape
```

```
{
  voidDraw();
}
class Circle : IShape
{
  private IColor color;
  public Circle(IColor color)
  {
    this.color = color;
  }
  public void Draw()
  {
    Console.WriteLine("Drawing a circle with color: " +color.GetColor());
  }
}
class Rectangle : IShape
{
  private IColor color;
  public Rectangle(IColor color)
  {
    this.color = color;
  }
```

```
  public void Draw()
  {
    Console.WriteLine("Drawing a rectangle with color: " +color.GetColor());
  }
}
interface IColor
{
  string GetColor();
}
class Red : IColor
{
  public string GetColor() => "Red";
}
class Blue : IColor
{
  public string GetColor() => "Blue";
}
class Program
{
  static void Main()
  {
    IShape redCircle = new Circle(new Red());
```

```
    IShape blueRectangle = new Rectangle(new Blue());
    redCircle.Draw();
    blueRectangle.Draw();
  }
}
```

In this example:

- IShape is the abstraction that defines the interface for shapes.
- Circle and Rectangle are refined abstractions that extend the IShape interface.
- IColor is the implementor that defines the interface for colors.
- Red and Blue are concrete implementors that provide specific implementations of the IColor interface.

The Bridge pattern allows you to change the implementation of a shape's color without affecting the shape itself. This makes the code more flexible and easier to maintain.

Explain Composite design pattern in C#.

The Composite pattern is a structural design pattern that composes objects into tree structures to represent part-whole hierarchies. It allows you to treat individual objects and compositions of objects uniformly.

Key Components:

- **Component:** Defines the interface for objects in the composition.
- **Leaf:** Represents leaf objects in the composition that have no children.
- **Composite:** Represents composite objects that can contain

other components.

Benefits of the Composite Pattern:

- **Uniformity:** Allows you to treat individual objects and compositions of objects uniformly.
- **Flexibility:** Makes it easy to add or remove components from the composition.
- **Reusability:** Can be used to create complex structures from simpler components.

The Composite pattern is a useful design pattern for representing hierarchical structures in your applications. It can be used to create flexible and maintainable code.

Example of Composite Pattern in C#.

```
interface IShape

{

  voidDraw();

}

class Circle : IShape

{

  public void Draw() => Console.WriteLine("Drawing acircle");

}

class Rectangle : IShape

{

  public void Draw() => Console.WriteLine("Drawing a rectangle");

}
```

```
class ShapeGroup : IShape
{
  private List<IShape> shapes = new List<IShape>();
   publicvoid Add(IShape shape) => shapes.Add(shape);
  public void Remove(IShape shape) => shapes.Remove(shape);
   public void Draw()
   {
     foreach (var shape in shapes)
     {
        shape.Draw();
     }
   }
}
class Program
{
  static void Main()
   {
     ShapeGroup group = new ShapeGroup();
     group.Add(new Circle());
     group.Add(new Rectangle());
     group.Add(new ShapeGroup()); // Can contain other groups
      group.Draw();
   }
```

```
}
```

In this example:

- IShape is the component interface.
- Circle and Rectangle are leaf objects.
- ShapeGroup is a composite object that can contain other shapes.

The ShapeGroup class implements the IShape interface and can contain both individual shapes and other groups of shapes. This allows you to treat both individual shapes and groups of shapes uniformly.

Explain Decorator design pattern in C#.

The Decorator pattern is a structural design pattern that attaches additional responsibilities to an object dynamically. This allows you to modify the behavior of an object without changing its class.

Key Components:

- **Component:** Defines the interface for objects that can be decorated.
- **ConcreteComponent:** Implements the component interface and represents the base object that can be decorated.
- **Decorator:** Implements the component interface and wraps a component object.
- **Concrete Decorators:** Extend the decorator class and provide specific additional responsibilities.

Benefits of the Decorator Pattern:

- **Flexibility:** Allows you to add new responsibilities to objects dynamically without modifying their classes.

- **Reusability:** Can be used to create reusable decorators that can be applied to different objects.
- **Extensibility:** Makes it easy to add new decorators to the system.

The Decorator pattern is a useful design pattern for adding additional behavior to objects without modifying their existing code. It is often used for features like logging, caching, or security.

Example of Decorator Pattern in C#.

```
interface IShape

{

  void Draw();

}

class Circle : IShape

{

  public void Draw() =>Console.WriteLine("Drawing a circle");

}

abstract classShapeDecorator : IShape

{

  protected IShape shape;

  public ShapeDecorator(IShape shape)

  {

    this.shape = shape;

  }

  public virtual void Draw() =>shape.Draw();
```

```
}
classRedBorderDecorator : ShapeDecorator
{
    public RedBorderDecorator(IShape shape) :base(shape) { }
    public override void Draw()
    {
        base.Draw();
        Console.WriteLine("Adding redborder");
    }
}
classThickBorderDecorator : ShapeDecorator
{
    public ThickBorderDecorator(IShape shape) :base(shape) { }
    public override void Draw()
    {
        base.Draw();
        Console.WriteLine("Adding thickborder");
    }
}
class Program
{
    static void Main()
    {
```

```
        IShape circle = new Circle();

        IShape redCircle = newRedBorderDecorator(circle);

        IShape thickRedCircle = newThickBorderDecorator(redCircle);

        thickRedCircle.Draw();

    }

}
```

In this example:

- IShape is the component interface.
- Circle is the concrete component.
- ShapeDecorator is the decorator base class.
- RedBorderDecorator and ThickBorderDecorator are concrete decorators that add specific responsibilities to the shape.

The ShapeDecorator class wraps the IShape object and provides a Draw method that can be overridden to add additional behavior. The RedBorderDecorator and ThickBorderDecorator classes extend the ShapeDecorator class and provide their own implementations of the Draw method to add red and thick borders, respectively.

Explain Facade design pattern in C#.

The Facade pattern is a structural design pattern that provides a unified interface to a set of interfaces in a subsystem. It hides the complexities of the subsystem and makes it easier for clients to use.

Key Components:

- **Facade:** Defines an interface that simplifies the interface of a subsystem.
- **Subsystem:** A group of classes that are part of the subsystem.

Benefits of the Facade Pattern:

- **Simplified interface:** Provides a simpler interface to a complex subsystem.
- **Loose coupling:** Decouples clients from the subsystem, making it easier to change the subsystem without affecting clients.
- **Encapsulation:** Encapsulates the complexity of the subsystem, making it easier to understand and maintain.

The Facade pattern is a useful design pattern for simplifying complex subsystems and making them easier to use. It can be used in various scenarios, such as providing a high-level API for a low-level subsystem or encapsulating a third-party library.

Example of Facade Pattern in C#.

```
interface IShape
{
  void Draw();
}
class Circle : IShape
{
  public void Draw() =>Console.WriteLine("Drawing a circle");
}
class Rectangle :IShape
{
  public void Draw() =>Console.WriteLine("Drawing a rectangle");
}
```

```
class Triangle :IShape
{
   public void Draw() =>Console.WriteLine("Drawing a triangle");
}
class  ShapeDrawer
{
   private IShape circle;
   private IShape rectangle;
   private IShape triangle;
   public ShapeDrawer()
   {
      circle = new Circle();
      rectangle = new Rectangle();
      triangle = new Triangle();
   }
   public void DrawCircle() =>circle.Draw();
   public void DrawRectangle() =>rectangle.Draw();
   public void DrawTriangle() =>triangle.Draw();
}
class Program
{
   static void Main()
   {
```

```
        ShapeDrawer drawer = new ShapeDrawer();
        drawer.DrawCircle();
        drawer.DrawRectangle();
        drawer.DrawTriangle();
    }
}
```

In this example:

- IShape is the interface for shapes.
- Circle, Rectangle, and Triangle are the concrete shapes.
- ShapeDrawer is the facade that provides a unified interface to the shapes.

The ShapeDrawer class hides the complexity of the shapes and provides a simpler interface for clients to use. This makes it easier to use the shapes without having to know their specific implementations.

Explain Flyweight design pattern in C#.

The Flyweight pattern is a structural design pattern that reduces the number of objects by sharing common data. It is often used when there are many objects with similar or identical states.

Key Components:

- **Flyweight:** Defines an interface for objects that can be shared.
- **Concrete Flyweight:** Implements the flyweight interface and represents a specific instance of the flyweight.
- **Flyweight Factory:** Creates and manages flyweight objects.

Benefits of the Flyweight Pattern:

- **Memory Efficiency:** Reduces memory usage by sharing common data.
- **Performance:** Can improve performance by avoiding unnecessary object creation.
- **Scalability:** Can handle large numbers of objects more efficiently.

The Flyweight pattern is a useful design pattern for situations where you need to create many similar objects. It can help to improve the performance and memory usage of your applications.

Example of Flyweight Pattern in C#.

```
interface IShape

{

  voidDraw(int x, int y);

}

class Circle : IShape

{

   private int radius;

   public Circle(int radius)

   {

      this.radius = radius;

   }

   public void Draw(int x, int y)

   {
```

```
        // Draw the circle at the specified coordinates
    }
}
class ShapeFactory
{
    private Dictionary<int, IShape>flyweights = new Dictionary<int,
IShape>();
    public IShape GetCircle(int radius)
    {
        if (!flyweights.ContainsKey(radius))
        {
            flyweights[radius] = newCircle(radius);
        }
        return flyweights[radius];
    }
}
class Program
{
    static void Main()
    {
        ShapeFactory factory = newShapeFactory();
        // Create multiple circles with the same radius
        IShape circle1 = factory.GetCircle(10);
```

```
        IShape circle2 = factory.GetCircle(10);
        IShape circle3 = factory.GetCircle(10);
        // All three circles will reference the same object
        Console.WriteLine(circle1 == circle2);// Output: True
        Console.WriteLine(circle2 == circle3);// Output: True
    }
}
```

In this example:

- IShape is the flyweight interface.
- Circle is the concrete flyweight.
- ShapeFactory is the flyweight factory that manages the creation and sharing of flyweight objects.

The ShapeFactory class uses a dictionary to store previously created circles based on their radius. When a new circle is requested, it checks if a circle with the same radius already exists and returns it if found. This avoids creating multiple instances of the same circle, saving memory.

Explain Proxy design pattern in C#.

The Proxy pattern is a structural design pattern that provides a surrogate or placeholder for another object to control access to it. It is often used to hide the complexity of an object or to add additional functionality to an existing object.

Key Components:

- **Subject:** Defines the interface for the real object.
- **Proxy:** Implements the subject interface and acts as a surrogate for the real object.

- **RealSubject:** Represents the real object.

Benefits of the Proxy Pattern:

- **Control access:** Allows you to control access to an object.
- **Lazy loading:** Can be used to delay the creation of an object until it is needed.
- **Caching:** Can be used to cache the results of an object's methods.
- **Remote proxy:** Can be used to provide a local interface to a remote object.

The Proxy pattern is a useful design pattern for adding additional functionality to objects without modifying their existing code. It can also be used to improve performance, security, or scalability.

Example of Proxy Pattern in C#.

```
interface IShape

{

  voidDraw();

}

class Circle : IShape

{

  public void Draw() => Console.WriteLine("Drawing acircle");

}

class ShapeProxy : IShape

{

  private IShape shape;
```

```
    public ShapeProxy(IShape shape)
    {
        this.shape = shape;
    }
    public void Draw()
    {
        Console.WriteLine("Starting to draw");
        shape.Draw();
        Console.WriteLine("Finished drawing");
    }
}
class Program
{
    static void Main()
    {
        IShape circle = new Circle();
        IShape proxy = new ShapeProxy(circle);
        proxy.Draw();
    }
}
```

In this example:

- IShape is the subject interface.
- Circle is the real subject.
- ShapeProxy is the proxy that provides additional functionality to the Circle object.

The ShapeProxy class wraps the Circle object and provides additional logging functionality before and after calling the Draw method. This allows you to control access to the Circle object and add additional behavior without modifying the Circle class itself.

Explain some of the Behavioral design pattern in C#.

Behavioral design patterns focus on how objects interact and communicate with each other. They address issues related to algorithms, object behavior, and communication. Here are some of the most commonly used behavioral patterns in C#:

Strategy Pattern

Purpose: Defines a family of algorithms, encapsulates each one, and makes them interchangeable.

Example:

```
interface IShape
{
  voidDraw();
}
class Circle : IShape
{
  public void Draw() => Console.WriteLine("Drawing acircle");
}
```

```
class Rectangle : IShape
{
  public void Draw() => Console.WriteLine("Drawing a rectangle");
}
class ShapeContext
{
  private IShape shape;
  public ShapeContext(IShape shape)
  {
    this.shape = shape;
  }
  public void Draw() => shape.Draw();
}
```

Observer Pattern

Purpose: Defines a one-to-many dependency between objects so that when one object changes state, all its dependents are notified and updated automatically.

Example:

```
interface ISubject
{
  voidAttach(IObserver observer);
  voidDetach(IObserver observer);
  voidNotify();
```

```
}
interface IObserver
{
  voidUpdate();
}
class ConcreteSubject : ISubject
{
  //...
}
class ConcreteObserver : IObserver
{
  //...
}
```

Iterator Pattern

Purpose: Provides a way to access the elements of an aggregate object sequentially without exposing its underlying representation.

Example:

```
interface IEnumerator<T>
{
  boolMoveNext();
  TCurrent { get; }
}
```

```
interface IEnumerable<T>
{
  IEnumerator<T> GetEnumerator();
}
```

Template Method Pattern

Purpose: Defines the skeleton of an algorithm in an operation, deferring some steps to subclasses.

Example:

```
abstract class Game
{
  public void Play()
  {
    Initialize();
    Rules();
    EndGame();
  }
  protected abstract void Initialize();
  protected abstract void Rules();
  protected abstract void EndGame();
}
```

CHAPTER 6

EXCEPTION HANDLING IN C#

What is the Exception in C#?

Exceptions in C# are a mechanism for handling unexpected errors or situations that occur during program execution. They provide a structured way to respond to errors and prevent your program from crashing.

Types of Exceptions:

- **System.Exception:** The base class for all exceptions in C#.
- **System.ApplicationException:** A derived class for application-specific exceptions.
- **System.SystemException:** A derived class for system-related exceptions.

Common Built-in Exceptions:

- **System.ArgumentException:** Thrown when an invalid argument is passed to a method.
- **System.NullReferenceException:** Thrown when you attempt to access a member of a null object.
- **System.IndexOutOfRangeException:** Thrown when an

index is outside the bounds of an array or collection.

- **System.DivideByZeroException:** Thrown when you attempt to divide a number by zero.
- **System.InvalidOperationException:** Thrown when an operation is invalid in the current context.

Exception Handling:

try-catch-finally Blocks:

```
try
{
  // Code that might throw an exception
}
catch (Exception ex)
{
  // Handle the exception
  Console.WriteLine("An error occurred: " + ex.Message);
}
finally
{
// Code that always executes, regardless of whether an exception is thrown
}
```

throw Statement:

```
throw new ArgumentException("Invalid argument");
```

Custom Exceptions:

You can create custom exceptions by deriving from Exception or ApplicationException. This allows you to provide more specific information about the error.

```
public class MyCustomException : Exception
{
    public MyCustomException(string message) : base(message)
    {
    }
}
```

Best Practices:

- **Catch specific exceptions:** Try to catch specific exceptions rather than the general Exception class to provide more targeted error handling.
- **Provide meaningful error messages:** Include informative messages in your exceptions to help with debugging.
- **Log exceptions:** Use a logging framework to record exceptions for analysis.
- **Avoid empty catch blocks:** Always provide appropriate handling for exceptions.

What are the Checked and Unchecked exceptions and the difference between them?

In C#, exceptions are classified into two categories: checked and unchecked. This distinction affects how the compiler handles them.

Checked Exceptions:

- **Compiler-Enforced:** The compiler requires you to either handle checked exceptions using a try-catch block or declare the method that throws them using the throws keyword.
- **Common Examples:** IOException, InvalidOperationException, ArgumentException
- **Purpose:** To ensure that potential exceptions are handled, preventing unexpected program termination.

Unchecked Exceptions:

- **Not Compiler-Enforced:** The compiler does not require you to handle unchecked exceptions.
- **Common Examples:** NullReferenceException, OutOfMemoryException, StackOverflowException
- **Purpose:** To represent runtime errors that are generally not recoverable.

Key Differences:

Feature	Checked Exceptions	Unchecked Exceptions
Compiler Enforcement	Enforced	Not enforced
Handling Requirement	Must be handled or declared	Optional
Typical Errors	Input/output errors, invalid operations	Runtime errors

Example:

try

```
{
  // Code that might throw a checked exception (e.g., FileNotFoundException)
}
catch (FileNotFoundException ex)
{
  // Handle the exception
}


// Unchecked exception (compiler doesn't require handling)
try
{
  int[] numbers = new int[0];
  numbers[1] = 10; // Will throw NullReferenceException
}
catch (NullReferenceException ex)
{
  // Handle the exception (optional)
}
```

Choosing Between Checked and Unchecked Exceptions:

- **Checked Exceptions:** Use checked exceptions when you want to force developers to handle potential errors and prevent unexpected program termination.
- **Unchecked Exceptions:** Use unchecked exceptions for

runtime errors that are generally not recoverable.

When and How you should create custom exceptions in C#?

When to Create Custom Exceptions:

- **Specific Error Conditions:** When you want to provide more specific information about an error than the built-in exceptions offer.
- **Custom Error Handling:** To implement custom error handling logic.
- **Domain-Specific Errors:** To define exceptions that are specific to your application domain.

How to Create Custom Exceptions:

Inherit from Exception or ApplicationException:

```
public class MyCustomException : Exception

{

  public MyCustomException(string message) : base(message)

  {

  }

}
```

1. **Provide a Constructor:**
   - The constructor can take additional parameters to provide more context about the exception.
2. **Add Properties or Methods:**
   - You can add custom properties or methods to your

exception class to store or retrieve additional information.

Example:

```
public class InvalidInputException : Exception
{
  public InvalidInputException(string message) : base(message)
  {
  }
  public string InvalidValue { get; set; }
}
```

Using Custom Exceptions:

Throw the exception:

```
if (input < 0)
{
throw new InvalidInputException("Input must be positive.");
}
```

Catch the exception:try

```
try
{
  // Code that might throw the exception
}
catch (InvalidInputException ex)
{
  Console.WriteLine("Invalid input: " + ex.Message);
```

}

Best Practices:

- **Provide informative messages:** Include clear and concise messages in your custom exceptions.
- **Consider inheritance:** If your custom exceptions have common properties or methods, you can create a base class and inherit from it.
- **Use a consistent naming convention:** Use a consistent naming convention for your custom exceptions.
- **Log exceptions:** Use a logging framework to record exceptions for analysis.

What is the purpose of the InnerException property?

The InnerException property in C# is used to get the root cause of an exception. It allows you to chain exceptions together, providing a clear hierarchy of related exceptions. This can help debug and understand the underlying causes of errors.

When to Use InnerException:

- **Nested Exceptions:** When one exception is thrown while handling another exception.
- **Custom Exception Handling:** To provide more context about the original exception that caused a custom exception to be thrown.
- **Debugging:** To trace the root cause of an exception and identify the source of the error.

Example:

try

```
{
  // Code that might throw an exception
}
catch (Exception ex)
{
  if (ex.InnerException != null)
  {
    Console.WriteLine("Inner exception: " + ex.InnerException.Message);
  }
  else
  {
    Console.WriteLine("Exception: " + ex.Message);
  }
}
```

In this example, if the original exception has an InnerException, the message of the inner exception is displayed. This can help identify the root cause of the error and provide more context for debugging.

Key Points:

- InnerException can be null if there is no underlying exception.
- You can chain multiple exceptions using the InnerException property.
- InnerException is often used in custom exception handling to provide more information about the error.

What is the difference between throw and throw ex;?

Both throw and throw ex; are used to rethrow exceptions in C#, but they have slightly different meanings:

- **throw:** When used without an expression, it rethrows the current exception without modifying it. This is typically used to propagate an exception up the call stack.

```
try

{

// Code that might throw an exception

}

catch (Exception ex)

{

throw; // Rethrows the original exception

}
```

- **throw ex;:** When used with an expression, it explicitly rethrows a specific exception object. This can be useful when you want to modify the exception before rethrowing it or create a new exception based on the original one.

```
try

{

// Code that might throw an exception

}

catch (Exception ex)

{

throw new CustomException("Custom error message", ex);
```

// Rethrows a new exception with the original exception as the inner exception

}

Key Differences:

Feature	`throw`	`throw ex;`
Rethrowing	Rethrows the current exception	Rethrows a specific exception object
Modification	Does not modify the exception	Can modify the exception before rethrowing
Usage	Typically used to propagate exceptions up the call stack	Used to rethrow a modified exception or create a new exception

What are some best practices for exception handling in C#?

Following are the best practices for exception handling in C#:

1. Catch Specific Exceptions: Avoid catching the generic Exception class unless necessary. Instead, catch specific exceptions to provide more targeted error handling.

2. Provide Meaningful Error Messages: Include informative messages in your exception messages to help with debugging and troubleshooting.

3. Log Exceptions: Use a logging framework like NLog or Serilog to record exceptions and their details for analysis.

4. Avoid Empty catch **Blocks:** Always provide appropriate handling for exceptions. Empty catch blocks can hide errors and make debugging difficult.

5. Consider Using try-finally **Blocks:** Use finally blocks to ensure that resources are properly disposed of, even if an exception occurs.

6. Use Custom Exceptions: Create custom exceptions to provide more specific information about errors in your application.

7. Avoid Nesting Too Many try-catch **Blocks:** Excessive nesting can make your code harder to read and maintain. Consider using a single try-catch block at a higher level and passing exceptions up the call stack.

8. Use using **Statements:** For objects that implement IDisposable, use a using statement to ensure that resources are properly disposed of, even if an exception occurs.

9. Consider Performance Implications: While exception handling is important, excessive use of exceptions can impact performance. Avoid throwing exceptions unnecessarily.

10. Test Your Exception Handling: Write unit tests to verify that your exception handling code works as expected.

How can you use exception filters to selectively catch exceptions?

Exception filters in C# provide a mechanism for selectively catching exceptions based on certain conditions. They allow you to fine-tune your exception handling logic and avoid unnecessary exception handling code.

Using Exception Filters:

Create an Exception Filter:

C#
```
bool MyExceptionFilter(Exception ex)

{

 // Filter condition

 return ex.GetType() == typeof(ArgumentNullException);

}
```

Apply the Exception Filter:

```
try
{
// Code that might throw an exception
}
catch (Exception ex) when (MyExceptionFilter(ex))
{
// Handle the exception if the filter condition is true
}
catch (Exception ex)
{
// Handle other exceptions
}
```

Example:

```
try
{
//Code that might throw an ArgumentNullException
}
catch (Exception ex) when (ex isArgumentNullException)
{
Console.WriteLine("ArgumentNullException caught!");
}
catch (Exception ex)
{
```

```
Console.WriteLine("Other exception caught: " + ex.Message);
}
```

Key Points:

- Exception filters are evaluated before the catch block is executed.
- The filter condition can be any boolean expression.
- You can have multiple catch blocks with different filters.
- Exception filters can be useful for conditionally handling exceptions based on their type or other criteria.

Use Cases:

- **Selective handling:** Catch only specific types of exceptions.
- **Performance optimization:** Avoid unnecessary exception handling by filtering out exceptions that don't need to be handled.
- **Custom exception handling:** Implement custom exception handling logic based on specific conditions.

What is exception chaining and how can it be useful?

Exception chaining is a technique in C# that allows you to link multiple exceptions together, creating a hierarchy of related exceptions. This can be useful for providing more context and information about the root cause of an error.

How to Implement Exception Chaining:

1. **Create a new exception:** Create a new exception object.
2. **Set the InnerException property:** Assign the original exception to the InnerException property of the new exception.

3. **Throw the new exception:** Throw the newly created exception.

Example:

```
try
{
// Code that might throw an exception
}
catch (Exception ex)
{
throw new CustomException("Custom error message", ex);
}
```

In this example, a CustomException is created with the original exception as its InnerException. This allows you to provide additional context or information about the error while preserving the original exception.

Benefits of Exception Chaining:

- **Provides more context:** Helps to understand the root cause of an exception by showing the chain of related exceptions.
- **Improved debugging:** Makes it easier to debug complex errors by tracing the exception hierarchy.
- **Customizable error handling:** Allows you to create custom exception hierarchies to suit your specific needs.

Example of using InnerException:

```
try
{
```

```
// Code that might throw an exception
}
catch (Exception ex)
{
if (ex.InnerException != null)
  {
Console.WriteLine("Inner exception: " +ex.InnerException.Message);
  }
else
  {
Console.WriteLine("Exception: " + ex.Message);
  }
}
```

How can you implement custom error handling mechanisms in C#?

Custom error handling mechanisms allow you to tailor exception handling to your specific application requirements. Here are some strategies:

1. Custom Exception Classes:

- Create custom exception classes that inherit from Exception or ApplicationException.
- Provide informative messages and additional properties to describe the error.

```
public class MyCustomException : Exception
```

```
{
public MyCustomException(string message) : base(message)
  {
  }
}
```

2. Exception Filters:

- Use exception filters to selectively catch exceptions based on certain conditions.

```
try
{
// Code that might throw an exception
}
catch (Exception ex) when (ex is ArgumentNullException)
{
// Handle ArgumentNullException specifically
}
```

3. Exception Chaining:

- Link multiple exceptions together using the InnerException property to provide more context.

```
throw new CustomException("Custom error message", innerException);
```

4. Logging:

- Use a logging framework (e.g., NLog, Serilog) to record

exceptions and their details.

```
try
{
// Code that might throw an exception
}
catch (Exception ex)
{
  logger.Error(ex, "An error occurred.");
}
```

5. Error Handling Patterns:

- **Retry Pattern:** Attempt to retry an operation if it fails due to transient errors.
- **Circuit Breaker Pattern:** Prevent cascading failures by isolating failing components.
- **Timeout Pattern:** Set timeouts for operations to prevent indefinite waiting.
- **Fallback Mechanism:** Provide alternative actions if an operation fails.

6. User-Friendly Error Messages:

- Provide clear and informative error messages to users.
- Avoid technical jargon and use language that is understandable to non-technical users.

7. Centralized Error Handling:

- Create a central error handling mechanism that can be used throughout your application.

Example of Custom Error Handling:

```
public class MyCustomException : Exception
{
public MyCustomException(string message) : base(message)
{
}
}


try
{
// Code that might throw an exception
}
catch (MyCustomException ex)
{
// Handle the custom exception
logger.Error(ex, "Custom exception occurred.");
// Provide a user-friendly error message
Console.WriteLine("An error occurred. Please try again.");
}
catch (Exception ex)
```

```
{
// Handle other exceptions
logger.Error(ex, "Unexpected error occurred.");
}
```

Chapter 7

Architectural Patterns

.NET Framework and Architectural Patterns

N-Tier Architecture

- **Definition:** A classic approach dividing applications into layers: presentation, business logic, and data access.
- **.NET Implementation:**
  - **Presentation Layer:** ASP.NET for web applications, Windows Forms or WPF for desktop applications.
  - **Business Logic Layer:** C# classes encapsulating business rules and logic.
  - **Data Access Layer:** ADO.NET for interacting with databases.
- **Benefits:** Clear separation of concerns, improved maintainability, and scalability.

Three-Tier Architecture

- **Definition:** A specific implementation of N-Tier, often used for web applications.

- **.NET Implementation:**
  - **Presentation Tier:** ASP.NET Web Forms or MVC.
  - **Business Logic Tier:** C# classes and WCF services.
  - **Data Access Tier:** ADO.NET or Entity Framework.
- **Benefits:** Scalability, flexibility, and improved security.

Service-Oriented Architecture (SOA)

- **Definition:** Building applications as a collection of services that communicate with each other.
- **.NET Implementation:**
  - **WCF:** For creating and consuming services.
  - **ASP.NET Web API:** For building HTTP-based services.
  - **Windows Communication Foundation (WCF):** For various messaging patterns.
- **Benefits:** Reusability, scalability, and flexibility.

Model-View-Controller (MVC)

- **Definition:** Separates an application into three interconnected parts: Model, View, and Controller.
- **.NET Implementation:**
  - **ASP.NET MVC:** Provides a framework for building web applications using MVC pattern.
  - **Model:** Represents data and business logic.
  - **View:** Defines the UI and user interactions.
  - **Controller:** Handles user input and interacts with the

model and view.

- **Benefits:** Improved code organization, testability, and maintainability.

Model-View-ViewModel (MVVM)

- **Definition:** Primarily used for WPF applications, separating UI from business logic.
- **.NET Implementation:**
  - **WPF:** Utilizes data binding and commands.
  - **Model:** Represents data.
  - **View:** Defines the UI.
  - **ViewModel:** Acts as a bridge between the model and view.
- **Benefits:** Improved testability, maintainability, and separation of concerns.

Onion Architecture with .NET Framework

Onion architecture is a layered architectural pattern that emphasizes the separation of concerns and testability. It's named due to its layered structure, resembling an onion.

Layers in Onion Architecture

- **Domain Layer**: The core of the application, containing entities, value objects, and domain services. It should be completely independent of any external dependencies.
- **Application Layer**: Contains application-specific business logic, orchestrating domain objects and defining use cases.
- **Infrastructure Layer**: Handles external dependencies like databases, messaging systems, and UI frameworks.

.NET Implementation

- **Domain Layer**:
  - C# classes representing domain entities and value objects.
  - Domain services for business logic that don't belong to entities.
- **Application Layer**:
  - C# interfaces defining application services.
  - Concrete implementations of application services.
  - Dependency injection to manage dependencies.
- **Infrastructure Layer**:
  - Entity Framework for data access.
  - HTTP clients for external services.
  - Logging and error handling implementations.

Key Principles

- **Dependency Inversion**: Outer layers depend on abstractions defined in inner layers.
- **Dependency Injection**: Use dependency injection to manage dependencies between layers.
- **Interfaces**: Define interfaces in the application layer to decouple components.
- **Testability**: High testability due to the isolation of layers.

Benefits of Onion Architecture:

- Improved maintainability: Changes in one layer have minimal impact on others.

- Enhanced testability: Easier to write unit tests due to isolation.
- Flexibility: Adaptable to different UI technologies and data access strategies.
- Reusability: Domain layer can be reused in different applications.

Example

- An Order entity in the domain layer.
- An IOrderService interface in the application layer.
- A concrete OrderService implementation in the infrastructure layer.
- An ASP.NET MVC controller using the OrderService to retrieve and display products.

Clean Architecture with .NET Framework

Clean architecture is a software architecture pattern that emphasizes the separation of concerns and testability. It's often visualized as an onion, with layers representing different levels of abstraction.

Layers in Clean Architecture

- **Entities:** This innermost layer defines the core business rules and objects. It should be completely independent of any external dependencies.
- **Use Cases:** This layer contains application-specific business logic that orchestrates the domain entities.
- **Interface Adapters:** This layer acts as an adapter between the inner layers and the outer layers. It includes controllers, presenters, and data access logic.

- **Frameworks and Drivers:** This outer layer contains the UI, databases, and other external dependencies.

.NET Implementation

- **Entities:** C# classes representing domain objects.
- **Use Cases:** C# classes encapsulating business logic using dependency injection.
- **Interface Adapters:**
  - ASP.NET MVC controllers for web applications.
  - Entity Framework for data access.
  - Other frameworks or libraries as needed.
- **Frameworks and Drivers:**
  - ASP.NET, Entity Framework, UI frameworks, etc.

Key Principles

- **Dependency Inversion:** Outer layers depend on abstractions defined in inner layers.
- **Dependency Injection:** Use dependency injection to manage dependencies between layers.
- **Interfaces:** Define interfaces in the use case layer to decouple components.
- **Testability:** High testability due to the isolation of layers.

Benefits of Clean Architecture

- **Improved maintainability:** Changes in one layer have minimal impact on others.

- **Enhanced testability:** Easier to write unit tests due to isolation.
- **Flexibility:** Adaptable to different UI technologies and data access strategies.
- **Reusability:** Domain layer can be reused in different applications.

Example

- An Order entity in the Entities layer.
- An IOrderService interface in the Use Cases layer.
- An OrderService implementation in the Interface Adapters layer using Entity Framework to access the database.
- An ASP.NET MVC controller using the OrderService to retrieve and display product information.

Onion Architecture vs. Clean Architecture

While both Onion Architecture and Clean Architecture share the core principle of separating concerns and achieving high testability, there are subtle differences in their approach and terminology.

Onion Architecture

- Emphasizes layers and dependencies flowing from the outer layers towards the inner core.
- Focuses on the physical structure of the application.
- Layers typically include:
    - Infrastructure (databases, UI frameworks)
    - Application (business logic, orchestration)

  - Domain (entities, value objects)

Clean Architecture

- Emphasizes the independence of the core business logic from external details.
- Focuses on the logical structure of the application.
- Layers typically include:
  - Entities (business rules)
  - Use Cases (application business logic)
  - Interface Adapters (controllers, presenters, data access)
  - Frameworks and Drivers (UI, databases, etc.)

Key Differences

- **Terminology**: While the concepts are similar, the naming of layers and components differs slightly.
- **Dependency Rule**: Both architectures follow the dependency rule (outer layers depend on inner layers), but the emphasis might vary.
- **Focus**: Onion architecture often emphasizes the physical structure, while Clean Architecture leans more toward the logical structure.

In essence,

Both Onion Architecture and Clean Architecture are effective approaches to building well-structured and maintainable applications. The choice between the two often comes down to personal preference and the specific needs of the project. Many developers find that the principles of both architectures can be combined to create a hybrid approach.

Hexagonal Architecture with .NET Framework

Hexagonal Architecture, also known as Ports and Adapters, is a design pattern focused on isolating the core business logic from external concerns. It promotes high testability, maintainability, and flexibility.

Core Components

- **Domain**: Contains the core business logic, entities, and value objects.
- **Application**: Defines the use cases and orchestrates the domain logic.
- **Ports**: Define the contracts between the application and external systems.
- **Adapters**: Implement the ports to interact with external systems (databases, UI, messaging).

.NET Implementation

- **Domain**: C# classes representing domain entities and value objects.
- **Application**: C# interfaces defining application services.
- **Ports**: C# interfaces defining contracts for external interactions (e.g., IUserRepository, IOrderRepository).
- **Adapters**:
  - **Infrastructure adapters**: Implement data access logic using Entity Framework or other ORMs.
  - **UI adapters**: Implement user interfaces using ASP.NET MVC, WPF, or other frameworks.
  - **External service adapters**: Implement communication with external systems (e.g., HTTP clients, message queues).

Key Benefits

- **Testability**: Easily mock external dependencies for unit testing.
- **Flexibility**: Can be adapted to different UI technologies and data access strategies.
- **Maintainability**: Clear separation of concerns improves code organization.
- **Reusability**: Domain layer can be reused in different contexts.

CHAPTER 8

SQL DATABASE

What is SQL?

SQL (Structured Query Language) is a domain-specific language used for communicating with and managing relational databases. It provides a standardized way to interact with databases, allowing you to:

- **Create, modify, and delete** database objects like tables, views, and indexes.
- **Retrieve data** from the database using queries.
- **Insert, update, and delete** data within tables.
- **Manage** database transactions and security.

Key SQL Components:

- **Data Definition Language (DDL):** Used to define database structures, such as creating, modifying, and deleting tables, indexes, and views.
- **Data Manipulation Language (DML):** Used to manipulate data within tables, including inserting, updating, and deleting records.
- **Data Control Language (DCL):** Used to manage user access and permissions.

Example of a simple SQL query:

SQL

SELECT * FROM Customers WHERE City = 'Delhi';

This query retrieves all customers from the Customers table where the City is 'Delhi'.

SQL Server Versions and details.

SQL Server 2022 (Release Date: November 1, 2022; EOL Date: January 11, 2033)

- **In-Memory OLTP:** Enhanced performance for transactional workloads.
- **Always On Availability Groups:** Improved availability and disaster recovery features.
- **JSON support:** Native support for JSON data types.
- **Machine Learning Services:** Built-in machine learning capabilities.
- **Graph Database:** Support for graph-based data modeling and querying.

SQL Server 2019 (Release Date: November 2, 2019; EOL Date: January 11, 2029)

- **Hybrid cloud capabilities:** Integration with Azure SQL Managed Instance.
- **Intelligent query processing:** Improved query optimization and performance.
- **Database auditing:** Enhanced auditing and security features.
- **Big data support:** Integration with Hadoop and Spark for big

data analytics.

SQL Server 2017 (Release Date: March 2, 2017; EOL Date: January 12, 2027)

- **Container support:** Deployment and management of SQL Server in containers.
- **Hybrid cloud integration:** Deeper integration with Azure services.
- **Machine learning:** Basic machine learning capabilities.
- **Always Encrypted:** Enhanced data encryption at rest and in motion.

SQL Server 2016 (Release Date: June 22, 2016; EOL Date: July 12, 2026)

- **In-memory OLTP:** Introduced for high-performance transactional workloads.
- **Always On Availability Groups:** Enhanced availability and disaster recovery features.
- **Polybase:** Integration with external data sources like Hadoop and Azure Data Lake Storage.
- **Stretch Database:** Offload cold data to Azure for cost optimization.

SQL Server 2014 (Release Date: April 1, 2014; EOL Date: July 9, 2024)

- **Columnstore indexes:** Optimized for analytical workloads.
- **AlwaysOn Availability Groups:** Introduced for high availability and disaster recovery.
- **Memory-Optimized tables:** Improved performance for

in-memory data storage and processing.

SQL Server 2012 (Release Date: March 7, 2012; EOL Date: July 12, 2022)

- **AlwaysOn Availability Groups:** Introduced for high availability and disaster recovery.
- **Columnstore indexes:** Introduced for analytical workloads.
- **Parallel Data Warehouse:** Introduced for large-scale data warehousing and analytics.

What is a database management system and how many types of DBMS are there?

A **Database Management System (DBMS)** is software that provides a structured way to store, manage, and retrieve data. It acts as an interface between the database and the end-user, handling tasks like data storage, retrieval, security, and concurrency control.

Types of DBMS:

1. **Relational Database Management System (RDBMS):**
   - Stores data in tables that are related to each other through keys and indexes.
   - Examples: SQL Server, MySQL, Oracle, PostgreSQL, SQLite
2. **NoSQL Databases:**
   - Designed for handling large volumes of unstructured or semi-structured data.
   - Examples: MongoDB, Cassandra, Redis, Couchbase
3. **Object-Oriented Database Management System (OODBMS):**

- Stores data as objects, allowing for complex relationships and inheritance.
- Examples: ObjectStore, Versant, GemStone

4. **Hierarchical Database Management System (HDDBMS):**
   - Stores data in a hierarchical structure, similar to a tree.
   - Examples: IMS, IDMS
5. **Network Database Management System (NDDBMS):**
   - Stores data in a network structure, allowing for more complex relationships than hierarchical databases.
   - Examples: CODASYL, IDMS

Choosing the Right DBMS:

The choice of DBMS depends on factors such as:

- **Data type:** Structured, semi-structured, or unstructured data.
- **Scalability:** The need to handle large volumes of data.
- **Performance:** The required speed of data access and retrieval.
- **Consistency:** The need for ACID (Atomicity, Consistency, Isolation, Durability) properties.
- **Cost:** The budget for the DBMS.

What is RDBMS (Relational Database Management System)?

RDBMS (Relational Database Management System) is a type of database management system that stores data in tables that are related to each other through keys and indexes. This structure allows for efficient data retrieval, manipulation, and storage.

Key characteristics of RDBMS:

- **Data organization:** Data is stored in tables, where each table represents a collection of related data.
- **Relationships:** Relationships between tables are defined using primary and foreign keys.
- **Normalization:** RDBMS typically follows normalization principles to ensure data integrity and avoid redundancy.
- **SQL:** Uses SQL (Structured Query Language) for data manipulation and retrieval.
- **Transactions:** Supports transactions to ensure data consistency and integrity.

What is normalization and denormalization in the database?

Normalization and **denormalization** are techniques used to optimize database design and performance.

Normalization

Normalization is the process of organizing data in a database to minimize redundancy and improve data integrity. It involves breaking down large tables into smaller, more focused tables and defining relationships between them.

Benefits of normalization:

- **Reduces redundancy:** Prevents duplication of data, saving storage space.
- **Enhances data integrity:** Ensures data consistency and accuracy.
- **Improves query performance:** Can optimize query execution

by reducing the amount of data that needs to be processed.

Normalization forms:

- **First Normal Form (1NF):** Each column in a table should contain atomic values (not repeating groups).
- **Second Normal Form (2NF):** A table is in 2NF if it is in 1NF and all non-key attributes are dependent on the entire primary key.
- **Third Normal Form (3NF):** A table is in 3NF if it is in 2NF and all non-key attributes are mutually independent.
- **Boyce-Codd Normal Form (BCNF):** A stricter form of 3NF, requiring that all non-key attributes are dependent on only one superkey.

Denormalization

Denormalization is the process of introducing redundancy into a database design to improve performance or simplify queries. It involves combining related data into a single table, even if it violates normalization rules.

Reasons for denormalization:

- **Performance optimization:** Can improve query performance for frequently accessed data.
- **Simplified queries:** Can simplify complex queries by reducing the number of joins required.
- **Data warehousing:** Often used in data warehouses to optimize reporting and analysis.

Trade-offs of denormalization:

- **Increased redundancy:** Can lead to data inconsistencies if not managed carefully.

- **Reduced data integrity:** May violate normalization rules and compromise data quality.

Choosing between normalization and denormalization:

The decision to normalize or denormalize a database depends on various factors, including:

- **Query patterns:** If you have frequently executed queries that involve joins, denormalization might improve performance.
- **Data volume:** For very large datasets, denormalization can help reduce the number of joins and improve query performance.
- **Update frequency:** If data is frequently updated, normalization can help maintain data integrity.

What are the different data types in SQL?

SQL databases support a variety of data types to represent different kinds of data. Here are some common data types found in most SQL databases:

Numeric Data Types

- **INTEGER (INT):** Stores whole numbers (e.g., 10, -5).
- **SMALLINT:** Stores smaller whole numbers (e.g., 2, -3).
- **TINYINT:** Stores very small whole numbers (e.g., 1, 0).
- **BIGINT:** Stores larger whole numbers (e.g., 9223372036854775807).
- **DECIMAL (or NUMERIC):** Stores precise decimal numbers (e.g., 3.14159).
- **FLOAT:** Stores approximate floating-point numbers (e.g.,

1.23456e7).

- **REAL:** Stores approximate floating-point numbers (smaller range than FLOAT).

Character Data Types

- **CHAR:** Stores fixed-length character strings (e.g., 'Hello').
- **VARCHAR:** Stores variable-length character strings (e.g., 'This is a longer string').
- **NCHAR:** Stores fixed-length Unicode character strings (e.g., ' □□').
- **NVARCHAR:** Stores variable-length Unicode character strings (e.g., 'This is a longer Unicode string').
- **TEXT (or CLOB):** Stores large character strings (e.g., long text descriptions).

Date and Time Data Types

- **DATE:** Stores a date (e.g., '2023-12-31').
- **TIME:** Stores a time (e.g., '10:30:00').
- **DATETIME:** Stores a date and time (e.g., '2023-12-31 10:30:00').
- **TIMESTAMP:** Stores a date, time, and time zone information.

Other Data Types

- **BINARY:** Stores binary data (e.g., images, files).
- **VARBINARY:** Stores variable-length binary data.
- **BOOLEAN (or BIT):** Stores a boolean value (true or false).

- **GUID (or UNIQUEIDENTIFIER):** Stores a globally unique identifier.

Explain the difference between DDL, DML, and DCL statements.

SQL (Structured Query Language) is divided into three main categories of statements:

Data Definition Language (DDL)

DDL statements are used to define the structure of a database. They are used to create, modify, and delete database objects like tables, indexes, views, and stored procedures.

Examples of DDL statements:

- **CREATE TABLE:** Creates a new table.
- **ALTER TABLE:** Modifies an existing table.
- **DROP TABLE:** Deletes a table.
- **CREATE INDEX:** Creates an index on a table.
- **DROP INDEX:** Deletes an index.
- **CREATE VIEW:** Creates a virtual table based on the result of a query.

Data Manipulation Language (DML)

DML statements are used to manipulate data within tables. They are used to insert, update, and delete data.

Examples of DML statements:

- **INSERT INTO:** Inserts new rows into a table.

- **UPDATE:** Modifies existing rows in a table.
- **DELETE:** Deletes rows from a table.
- **SELECT:** Retrieves data from tables.

Data Control Language (DCL)

DCL statements are used to manage user access and permissions.

Examples of DCL statements:

- **GRANT:** Grants privileges to a user or role.
- **REVOKE:** Revokes privileges from a user or role.
- **DENY:** Denies privileges to a user or role.

What is ACID?

ACID is a set of properties that ensure data integrity and consistency in a database system. It stands for:

- **Atomicity:** A transaction is either executed entirely or not at all. If any part of the transaction fails, the entire transaction is rolled back to its original state.
- **Consistency:** The database must be in a consistent state before and after a transaction. This means that all constraints and rules are enforced.
- **Isolation:** Transactions should not interfere with each other. Each transaction should appear to be the only transaction running in the system.
- **Durability:** Once a transaction is committed, its changes are permanent and should survive system failures.

These properties are essential for ensuring the reliability and correctness of database operations.

What are the constraints in SQL? Explain in detail.

Constraints in SQL are rules or limitations imposed on data to maintain its accuracy and consistency. They help prevent errors and inconsistencies in the database. There are several types of constraints commonly used in SQL:

1. NOT NULL: Ensures that a column cannot contain null values.

Example:

```
CREATE TABLE Customers (
  CustomerID INT PRIMARY KEY,
  CustomerName VARCHAR(50) NOT NULL,
  ContactNumber VARCHAR(20) NOT NULL
);
```

This prevents customers from being created without a name or contact number.

2. UNIQUE: Guarantees that all values in a column must be unique.

Example:

```
CREATE TABLE Orders (
  OrderID INT PRIMARY KEY,
  OrderNumber INT UNIQUE
);
```

No two orders can have the same order number.

3. PRIMARY KEY: Identifies a unique row in a table. It is a combination of NOT NULL and UNIQUE constraints.

Example:

```
CREATE TABLE Products (
```

```
  ProductID INT PRIMARY KEY,
  ProductName VARCHAR(50),
  Price DECIMAL(10, 2)
);
```

The ProductID column uniquely identifies each product.

4. FOREIGN KEY: Defines a relationship between two tables, ensuring data integrity. It references a primary key in another table.

Example:

```
CREATE TABLE OrderDetails (
  OrderID INT,
  ProductID INT,
  Quantity INT,
  PRIMARY KEY (OrderID, ProductID),
  FOREIGN KEY (OrderID) REFERENCES Orders(OrderID),
  FOREIGN KEY (ProductID) REFERENCES Products(ProductID)
);
```

This establishes a relationship between the OrderDetails table and the Orders and Products tables, ensuring that only valid order and product IDs are used.

5. CHECK: Enforces a condition on the data that must be met for a row to be inserted or updated.

Example:

```
CREATE TABLE Employees (
  EmployeeID INT PRIMARY KEY,
```

```
  Salary DECIMAL(10, 2) CHECK (Salary >= 10000)
);
```

This ensures that the salary of an employee is always greater than or equal to 10000.

6. DEFAULT: Specify a default value for a column if no value is provided during insertion.

Example:

```
CREATE TABLE Orders (
  OrderID INT PRIMARY KEY,
  OrderDate DATE DEFAULT GETDATE()
);
```

If no order date is specified, the current date will be used as the default.

By using these constraints, you can maintain the quality and reliability of your database data.

Difference between primary key and unique key.

The primary key and unique key constraints in SQL serve similar purposes but have some key differences:

Primary Key:

- **Uniqueness:** Ensures that all values in the column are unique.
- **Non-Null:** Cannot contain null values.
- **Identifier:** Acts as a unique identifier for each row in the table.
- **One per table:** A table can have only one primary key.
- **Clustering index:** Often used to create a clustering index, which can improve query performance.

Unique Key:

- **Uniqueness:** Ensures that all values in the column or combination of columns are unique.
- **Can contain null values:** Can allow null values.
- **No identifier:** Does not necessarily identify a row uniquely.
- **Multiple per table:** A table can have multiple unique keys.
- **No clustering index:** Does not automatically create a clustering index.

Key points to remember:

- A primary key is always a unique key, but a unique key is not always a primary key.
- A table can have only one primary key, but it can have multiple unique keys.
- The primary key is often used to create a clustering index, while the unique key does not automatically create a clustering index.

What is Composite Key?

A composite key is a primary key that consists of multiple columns. Unlike a simple primary key, which is composed of a single column, a composite key uses a combination of columns to uniquely identify a row in a table.

Why use a composite key?

- **Unique identification:** Composite keys provide a reliable way to uniquely identify rows in a table, even when individual columns may not be unique.
- **Relationships:** They can be used to represent relationships

between entities in a database.

- **Data integrity:** Composite keys help maintain data integrity by preventing duplicate or inconsistent data.

Important considerations:

- **Performance:** Using a composite key can affect query performance, especially if the columns involved are not indexed or if the queries frequently involve filtering on the composite key.
- **Updates:** Updating a column that is part of a composite key can be more complex, as it may require updating related rows in other tables.
- **Design:** Carefully consider the columns to include in a composite key to ensure that it effectively identifies rows and maintains data integrity.

What is an Identity Column?

Identity Columns in SQL are columns that automatically generate unique values for each new row inserted into a table. These values are typically sequential numbers, but can also be other data types like GUIDs.

Key characteristics of identity columns:

- **Automatic generation:** The database system automatically generates a unique value for each new row.
- **Sequential values:** By default, identity columns generate sequential numbers.
- **Data type:** Can be of various data types, including INT, BIGINT, SMALLINT, and uniqueidentifiers (GUIDs).
- **Seed and increment values:** You can specify the starting value (seed) and the increment between values.

Syntax:

```
CREATE TABLE [TableName] (
[ColumnName] IDENTITY(seed, increment) [DataType]
);
```

Example:

```
CREATE TABLE Customers (
  CustomerID INT IDENTITY(1,1),
  CustomerName VARCHAR(50),
  ContactNumber VARCHAR(20)
);
```

In this example, the CustomerID column is an identity column that will automatically generate sequential numbers starting from 1 with an increment of 1 for each new customer added.

Uses of identity columns:

- **Primary keys:** Identity columns are often used as primary keys to uniquely identify rows in a table.
- **Sequencing:** They can be used to sequence records in a table, such as order numbers or invoice numbers.
- **Auditing:** Identity columns can be used for auditing purposes to track changes to data over time.

Re-seed the column:

This method sets the identity column's seed value to a new value, effectively resetting its starting point.

ALTER TABLE [TableName] ALTER COLUMN [ColumnName] IDENTITY(new_seed_value, increment_value);

To **enable or disable identity insert** in SQL Server, you can use the following commands:

-- Enable identity insert for the Customers table SET IDENTITY_INSERT Customers ON;

-- Insert a new row with a specific CustomerID

INSERT INTO Customers (CustomerID, CustomerName, ContactNumber) VALUES (1000, 'John Doe', '1234567890');

-- Disable identity insert

SET IDENTITY_INSERT Customers OFF;

Difference between Delete and Truncate.

Both DELETE and TRUNCATE statements are used to remove data from a table in SQL, but they have distinct characteristics and implications:

DELETE Statement

- **Functionality:** Removes specific rows from a table based on a condition.
- **Impact:** Can be rolled back in a transaction.
- **Speed:** Generally slower than TRUNCATE, especially for large tables.
- **Triggers:** Triggers associated with the table are fired.

Syntax:DELETE FROM [TableName]

WHERE [Condition];

TRUNCATE TABLE Statement

- **Functionality:** Removes all rows from a table without affecting the table structure.
- **Impact:** Cannot be rolled back in a transaction.
- **Speed:** Significantly faster than DELETE for large tables.
- **Triggers:** Triggers are not fired.

Syntax:TRUNCATE TABLE [TableName];

Key Differences:

Feature	DELETE	TRUNCATE TABLE
Rows Removed	Specific rows based on a condition	All rows
Transaction Support	Can be rolled back	Cannot be rolled back
Speed	Slower	Faster
Triggers	Fires triggers	Does not fire triggers
Table Structure	Remains unchanged	Remains unchanged

When to Use Which:

- **DELETE:** Use when you want to remove specific rows based on a condition and need the ability to roll back the changes.
- **TRUNCATE TABLE:** Use when you need to quickly remove all rows from a table and don't need the ability to roll back the changes. This is often used for performance optimization or data cleanup.

Caution:

- Be cautious when using TRUNCATE TABLE as it is irreversible. Always consider the potential consequences before executing this statement.

- For large tables, using TRUNCATE TABLE can significantly improve performance compared to DELETE. However, the choice should be made based on your specific requirements and the need for data integrity.

Can we truncate table which has a foreign key?

No, you cannot directly truncate a table that has foreign key constraints.

Truncating a table removes all rows from it, which can lead to inconsistencies if there are foreign key references to that table. A foreign key constraint ensures that the values in a column of one table must match the values in a primary key or unique key of another table. If you truncate the table with the primary or unique key, the foreign key references in the other tables will become invalid, leading to data integrity errors.

To safely truncate a table with foreign key constraints, you have two options:

1. **Disable foreign key constraints:** Temporarily disable the foreign key constraints before truncating the table, and then re-enable them afterward. This will prevent foreign key errors during the truncation process.
2. **Use a DELETE statement:** Instead of TRUNCATE, use a DELETE statement with a WHERE clause to remove all rows from the table. This will allow you to delete rows while respecting the foreign key constraints.

Here's an example of how to disable foreign key constraints before truncating a table and then re-enable them:

ALTER TABLE [TableName] NOCHECK CONSTRAINT ALL;

TRUNCATE TABLE [TableName];

ALTER TABLE [TableName] CHECK CONSTRAINT ALL;

What are joins in SQL? Explain different types of joins.

Joins are used to combine rows from two or more tables based on a related column between them. They are essential for retrieving data from multiple tables in a relational database.

Types of Joins

1. INNER JOIN: Returns rows that have matching values in both tables.

Syntax:SELECT column_name(s)

FROM table1

INNER JOIN table2

ON table1.column_name = table2.column_name;

2. LEFT JOIN: Returns all rows from the left table, even if there are no matches in the right table.

Syntax:SELECT column_name(s)

FROM table1

LEFT JOIN table2

ON table1.column_name = table2.column_name;

3. RIGHT JOIN: Returns all rows from the right table, even if there are no matches in the left table.

Syntax:SELECT column_name(s)

FROM table1

RIGHT JOIN table2

ON table1.column_name = table2.column_name;

4. FULL OUTER JOIN: Returns all rows when there is a match in either left or right table.

Syntax:SELECT column_name(s)

FROM table1

FULL OUTER JOIN table2

ON table1.column_name = table2.column_name;

5. CROSS JOIN: Returns the Cartesian product of all rows from both tables.

Syntax:SELECT column_name(s)

FROM table1

CROSS JOIN table2;

What are the Functions in SQL?

Functions in SQL are predefined routines that perform specific tasks on data. They can be used to manipulate data, perform calculations, aggregate data, and more.

Types of Functions

1. **Scalar Functions:** Return a single value for each row.
    - **Mathematical functions:** ABS, CEILING, FLOOR, ROUND, SQRT, POWER, etc.
    - **String functions:** LEN, UPPER, LOWER, CONCAT, SUBSTRING, REPLACE, etc.
    - **Date and time functions:** DATEADD, DATEDIFF, GETDATE, MONTH, YEAR, etc.

- **System functions:** USER_NAME, CURRENT_TIMESTAMP, SERVERPROPERTY, etc.

2. **Aggregate Functions:** Return a single value for a group of rows.
   - COUNT: Returns the number of rows.
   - SUM: Calculates the sum of values.
   - AVG: Calculates the average of values.
   - MIN: Returns the minimum value.
   - MAX: Returns the maximum value.
3. **Window Functions:** Perform calculations over a set of rows that are related to the current row.
   - RANK: Assigns a rank to each row within a group.
   - DENSE_RANK: Assigns a rank to each row within a group, without gaps.
   - ROW_NUMBER: Assigns a sequential number to each row within a group.
   - LEAD: Accesses the value of a column in a following row.
   - LAG: Accesses the value of a column in a preceding row.

Scalar Function:

```
SELECT LEN(CustomerName) AS NameLength

FROM Customers;
```

Aggregate Function:

```
SELECT AVG(OrderAmount) AS AverageOrderAmount

FROM Orders;
```

Window Function:

SELECT CustomerID, OrderID, RANK() OVER (PARTITION BY CustomerID ORDER BY OrderDate DESC) AS OrderRank

FROM Orders;

User-Defined Functions: You can also create your own functions to encapsulate complex logic.

Example:

CREATE FUNCTION CalculateDiscount(@OrderAmountDECIMAL(10, 2))

RETURNS DECIMAL(10, 2)

AS

BEGIN

DECLARE @Discount DECIMAL(10, 2);

IF@OrderAmount > 1000

SET @Discount = @OrderAmount * 0.10;

ELSE

SET @Discount = 0;

RETURN @Discount;

END;

Functions are a powerful tool in SQL, allowing you to perform complex operations on your data in a concise and reusable manner.

What are Table Valued Functions?

Table-Valued Functions (TVFs) in SQL are functions that return a result set instead of a single value. They are similar to views but provide more flexibility.

Types of TVFs

1. **Scalar-Valued TVFs:**
   - Return a single column of data.
   - Can be used in places where a scalar value is expected, like in WHERE or JOIN clauses.
2. **Inline TVFs:**
   - Defined within a SELECT statement.
   - Provide a way to create temporary tables on the fly.
3. **Table TVFs:**
   - Defined separately from the SELECT statement.
   - Can be used in places where a table is expected, like in JOIN or INSERT statements.

Example: Scalar-Valued TVF

```
CREATE FUNCTION GetCustomersByCity(@CityVARCHAR(50))

RETURNS TABLE

AS

RETURN

 SELECT CustomerID, CustomerName

  FROMCustomers

  WHERE City =@City;
```

Example: Inline TVF

```
SELECT *
```

```
FROM Orders
JOIN (
  SELECT ProductID, ProductName
   FROMProducts
  WHERE ProductCategory = 'Electronics'
) AS Electronics ON Orders.ProductID =Electronics.ProductID;
```

Example: Table TVF

```
CREATE FUNCTION GetTopCustomers()
RETURNS TABLE
AS
RETURN
  SELECT TOP 10 CustomerID, CustomerName, TotalSales
   FROM(
    SELECT Customers.CustomerID, Customers.CustomerName,SUM(Orders.OrderAmount) AS TotalSales
    FROM Customers
    INNER JOIN Orders ON Customers.CustomerID = Orders.CustomerID
    GROUP BY Customers.CustomerID, Customers.CustomerName
   ) ASCustomerSales
   ORDER BYTotalSales DESC;
```

Key Benefits of TVFs:

- **Modularity:** Encapsulate complex logic into reusable functions.
- **Performance:** Can improve performance by avoiding multiple joins or subqueries.
- **Flexibility:** Can be used in various contexts, like queries, stored procedures, and other TVFs.
- **Readability:** Improve code readability by breaking down complex logic into smaller, more manageable units.

What are Stored Procedures?

Stored Procedures in SQL are precompiled sets of SQL statements that are stored on the database server. They provide a way to encapsulate complex database logic and improve performance.

Benefits of Stored Procedures

- **Performance:** Stored procedures are precompiled, which means they execute faster than executing individual SQL statements.
- **Modularity:** They can be used to break down complex database operations into smaller, reusable units.
- **Security:** Stored procedures can be used to implement security measures by restricting access to specific database objects or operations.
- **Reusability:** Stored procedures can be called multiple times from different applications or other stored procedures.
- **Maintainability:** Stored procedures can make it easier to maintain and update database code.

Syntax

```
CREATE PROCEDURE[schema_name].[procedure_name]
  @parameter1 datatype,
  @parameter2 datatype,
   ...
AS
BEGIN
  --SQL statements
END;
```

Example

```
CREATE PROCEDURE GetCustomersByCity
  @City VARCHAR(50)
AS
BEGIN
  SELECT CustomerID, CustomerName
   FROMCustomers
  WHERE City = @City;
END;
```

Calling a Stored Procedure

```
EXEC GetCustomersByCity @City = 'Delhi';
```

Types of Stored Procedures

- **System Stored Procedures:** Predefined procedures provided by the database system.
- **User-Defined Stored Procedures:** Created by database users.

Additional Features

- **Parameters:** Stored procedures can accept input parameters and return output parameters.
- **Temporary Tables:** They can create and use temporary tables for intermediate calculations.
- **Error Handling:** Stored procedures can include error handling mechanisms to handle exceptions.
- **Transactions:** They can be used to group multiple SQL statements into a single transaction.

Difference between Stored Procedures and Functions in SQL.

Key Differences

Feature	Stored Procedure	Function
Purpose	Complex operations	Single value or result set
Return Value	Multiple result sets or single result set	Single value or result set
Paramet ers	Input and output parameters	Input parameters only
Side Effects	Can modify database state.	Generally, avoid modifying the database state
Usage	Business logic, data manipulation	Calculations, data retrieval, validation

In summary:

- **Stored procedures** are more versatile and can perform a wider range of tasks, while **functions** are more specialized for returning specific values or result sets.

- **Stored procedures** are often used for business logic and data manipulation, while **functions** are commonly used for calculations and data retrieval.

How functions can modify the database state?

Functions cannot directly modify the database state. This is a fundamental difference between functions and stored procedures.

However, functions can indirectly modify the database state in certain ways:

1. **Calling Stored Procedures:** A function can call a stored procedure, which can then modify the database state.
2. **Triggering Rules or Constraints:** If a function is used in a trigger or constraint, and that trigger or constraint modifies the database state, the function can be said to have indirectly influenced the modification.
3. **Returning Values for Updates:** A function can return a value that is used to update a database table, indirectly modifying the state.

Can a function call a store procedure?

Yes, a function can call a stored procedure. This allows you to break down complex logic into smaller, more manageable units and reuse code.

Here's a basic example:

SQL

```
CREATE FUNCTIONCalculateTotalOrderAmount(@OrderID INT)

RETURNS DECIMAL(10, 2)

AS

BEGIN
```

```
DECLARE @TotalAmount DECIMAL(10, 2);
 --Call a stored procedure to get the order details
 EXECGetOrderDetails @OrderID = @OrderID;
 --Calculate the total amount based on the order details
SELECT @TotalAmount = SUM(Quantity * UnitPrice)
 FROMOrderDetails
WHERE OrderID = @OrderID;
 RETURN @TotalAmount;
END;
```

In this example, the CalculateTotalOrderAmount function calls the GetOrderDetails stored procedure to retrieve the order details. It then calculates the total amount based on the retrieved data and returns the result.

This approach can be beneficial for:

- **Modularity:** Breaking down complex logic into smaller, reusable units.
- **Performance:** Reusing precompiled stored procedures can improve performance.
- **Maintainability:** Simplifying the code and making it easier to understand and modify.

However, it's important to use this technique judiciously, as excessive function calls can sometimes impact performance. If the logic within the stored procedure is relatively simple and frequently used, it might be more efficient to include it directly within the function.

What is CTE?

Common Table Expressions (CTEs) are temporary result sets that are defined within a SELECT statement. They allow you to create complex queries in a more readable and maintainable way.

Syntax

```
WITH CTE_Name AS (
  SELECT column_name(s)
   FROMtable_name
  WHERE condition
)
SELECT column_name(s)
FROM CTE_Name;
```

Benefits of CTEs

- **Improved Readability:** CTEs can make complex queries easier to understand by breaking them down into smaller, more manageable parts.
- **Reusability:** A CTE can be referenced multiple times within a query, which can reduce redundancy and improve performance.
- **Recursion:** CTEs can be used to implement recursive queries, which are useful for hierarchical data structures.

Example: Recursive CTE: To recursively traverse the employee hierarchy to determine the level of each employee.

```
WITH RecursiveCTE AS (
  SELECT EmployeeID, ManagerID, Level
```

```
FROMEmployees
WHERE ManagerID IS NULL

UNION ALL

SELECT E.EmployeeID, E.ManagerID, R.Level + 1
FROMEmployees E
INNER JOIN RecursiveCTE R ON E.ManagerID = R.EmployeeID
)
SELECT EmployeeID, Level
FROM RecursiveCTE;
```

Example: Non-Recursive CTE: To calculate the total sales for each product.

```
WITH SalesData AS (
SELECT OrderID, ProductID, Quantity, UnitPrice
FROM Orders
INNER JOIN OrderDetails ON Orders.OrderID = OrderDetails.OrderID
)
SELECT ProductID, SUM(Quantity * UnitPrice) ASTotalSales
FROM SalesData
GROUP BY ProductID;
```

Explain Temp Table.

Temporary Tables in SQL are temporary result sets that are created within a session and are automatically dropped when the session ends. They are often used to store intermediate results or to perform complex calculations.

Types of Temporary Tables

1. **Local Temporary Tables:** Created within a stored procedure or function. They are only visible within that scope.
2. **Global Temporary Tables:** Created within a session and are visible to all objects within that session.

Local Temporary Table:

```
CREATE TABLE #TableName (
  column_name1 datatype,
  column_name2 datatype,
   ...
);
```

Global Temporary Table:

```
CREATE TABLE ##TableName (
  column_name1 datatype,
  column_name2 datatype,
   ...
);
```

What are table variables in SQL?

Table Variables in SQL are temporary tables that are created within a batch, stored procedure, or function. They are similar to temporary tables, but they have a few key differences:

- **Scope:** Table variables are only visible within the scope where they are declared. This means they are not visible outside of the stored procedure, function, or batch where they are created.
- **Performance:** Table variables can sometimes offer better performance than temporary tables, especially when used within stored procedures.
- **Syntax:** Table variables use the DECLARE keyword to declare their structure.

Syntax

```
DECLARE @TableName TABLE (
  column_name1 datatype,
  column_name2 datatype,
   ...
);
```

Differences between table variables and temporary tables.

Both table variables and temporary tables are used to store temporary data in SQL, but they have some key differences:

Scope

- **Table Variables:** Limited to the scope where they are declared (e.g., within a stored procedure, function, or batch).
- **Temporary Tables:** Can be used within a broader context, such as within a session or even across sessions if declared as

global temporary tables.

Performance

- **Table Variables:** Generally considered to have better performance than temporary tables, especially when used within stored procedures.
- **Temporary Tables:** Can still be efficient, but may have some overhead due to their broader scope.

Syntax

- **Table Variables:** Use the DECLARE keyword to declare their structure.
- **Temporary Tables:** Use the CREATE TABLE keyword to create them.

Creation and Dropping

- **Table Variables:** Automatically dropped when the scope where they are declared ends.
- **Temporary Tables:** Automatically dropped at the end of the session unless explicitly dropped using DROP TABLE.

Usage

- **Table Variables:** Often used for intermediate calculations within stored procedures or functions.
- **Temporary Tables:** Can be used for a wider range of purposes, such as storing intermediate results, creating temporary views, or performing complex data manipulations.

In summary:

- **Table variables** are more tightly scoped and often offer better performance, making them suitable for temporary data storage within specific contexts.
- **Temporary tables** provide a more flexible and reusable approach for storing temporary data, but may have some performance overhead.

What is a view in SQL?

Views in SQL are virtual tables that present a subset of data from one or more underlying tables. They provide a way to simplify complex queries and enhance data security.

Key Characteristics of Views

- **Virtual Tables:** Views do not store actual data. They present a customized view of existing data.
- **Query Definitions:** They are defined by a SELECT statement, specifying the columns and conditions for the view.
- **Data Security:** Views can be used to restrict access to specific data or columns.
- **Performance:** Views can improve performance by caching query results or by optimizing query execution.

Types of Views

- **Simple Views:** Based on a single table.
- **Complex Views:** Based on multiple tables, often using joins.
- **Indexed Views:** Views with indexes created on them, improving query performance.

- **Materialized Views:** Precomputed views that store the actual data, providing faster query results but requiring more maintenance.

Example

CREATE VIEW CustomersWithOrders AS

SELECT Customers.CustomerID, Customers.CustomerName, Orders.OrderID

FROM Customers

INNER JOIN Orders ON Customers.CustomerID = Orders.CustomerID;

This view presents a list of customers and their associated orders.

Indexed Views are views that have indexes created on them. These indexes are used to optimize query performance, similar to indexes on regular tables.

Example:

CREATE VIEW CustomersWithOrders AS

SELECT Customers.CustomerID, Customers.CustomerName, Orders.OrderID

FROM Customers

INNER JOIN Orders ON Customers.CustomerID = Orders.CustomerID;

CREATE INDEX IX_CustomersWithOrders_CustomerID ON CustomersWithOrders (CustomerID);

Materialized Views are precomputed views that store the actual data instead of presenting a virtual view. This can significantly improve query performance, especially for complex queries or large datasets.

Example:

CREATE MATERIALIZED VIEW CustomersWithTotalOrders AS

SELECT Customers.CustomerID, Customers.CustomerName, COUNT(Orders.OrderID) AS TotalOrders

FROM Customers

INNER JOIN Orders ON Customers.CustomerID = Orders.CustomerID

GROUP BY Customers.CustomerID, Customers.CustomerName;

Benefits of Views

- **Simplified Queries:** Views can make complex queries easier to write and understand.
- **Data Security:** Views can be used to restrict access to sensitive data.
- **Data Consistency:** Views can ensure data consistency by enforcing constraints.
- **Performance:** Indexed views can improve query performance.

Limitations of Views

- **Dependency on Underlying Tables:** If the underlying tables change, the view may need to be updated.
- **Performance Overhead:** Creating and maintaining views can sometimes add overhead.

Can we insert data in a table using views?

While directly inserting data into a view isn't possible, there are ways to achieve it. You can insert data in a table using views, provided all the not null columns of the table have values in the insert statement and the view is a simple view.

What are triggers in SQL?

Triggers are special stored procedures that automatically execute in response to specific events that occur on a database object. They offer a powerful way to automate tasks, enforce data integrity, and implement custom business logic within your SQL Server environment.

Types of Triggers

Based on the event they respond to, triggers fall into three main categories:

1. **Data Manipulation Language (DML) Triggers:**
   - Most common type of trigger.
   - Respond to INSERT, UPDATE, or DELETE statements on a table.
2. **Data Definition Language (DDL) Triggers:**
   - Less prevalent than DML triggers.
   - Respond to schema changes on a database or table, such as CREATE, ALTER, or DROP statements.
   - Useful for maintaining data integrity during schema modifications or enforcing specific schema rules.
3. **Logon Triggers:**
   - Executed when a user attempts to log in to the SQL Server instance.
   - Primarily used for security purposes, such as:
     - Auditing login attempts.

- Enforcing password policies.
- Restricting access based on login time.

Syntax:

```
CREATE [ OR ALTER ] TRIGGER [ schema_name .]trigger_name
ON { table | view }
[ WITH <dml_trigger_option> [ ,...n ]] □
{ FOR | AFTER | INSTEAD OF }
{ [ INSERT ] [ , ] [ UPDATE ] [ , ] [ DELETE ]} □
[ WITH APPEND ]
[ NOT FOR REPLICATION ]
AS { sql_statement [ ; ] [ ,...n ] | EXTERNAL NAME <method specifier
[ ; ] > }

<dml_trigger_option> ::=
  [ENCRYPTION ]
  [EXECUTE AS Clause ]

<method_specifier> ::=
 assembly_name.class_name.method_name
```

What are inserted and deleted tables in SQL?

Inserted and Deleted Tables are special temporary tables automatically created by SQL Server when triggers are executed. They contain the rows that are affected by the DML (Data Manipulation Language) statement that triggered the event.

Inserted Table

- Contains the **new** rows that were inserted or updated by the DML statement.
- Can be used to access the values of the new data.

Deleted Table

- Contains the **old** rows that were deleted or updated by the DML statement.
- Can be used to access the values of the original data.

Example:

```
CREATE TRIGGER trg_UpdateOrderTotal
ON OrderDetails
AFTER UPDATE
AS
BEGIN
  UPDATE Orders
    SETTotalAmount = SUM(OrderDetails.Quantity * OrderDetails.UnitPrice)
   FROMOrders
  INNER JOIN inserted ON Orders.OrderID = inserted.OrderID;
END;
```

In this trigger, the inserted table contains the new values of the updated OrderDetails rows, while the deleted table would contain the old values of those rows.

Using Inserted and Deleted Tables

- **Calculating Differences:** Compare the values in the inserted and deleted tables to determine the changes made by the DML statement.
- **Enforcing Business Rules:** Implement complex business

rules based on the values in the inserted and deleted tables.

- **Auditing Changes:** Log changes to the database by inserting data from the inserted and deleted tables into an audit table.

Important Notes:

- The inserted and deleted tables are only available within the context of the trigger. They cannot be accessed outside of the trigger's scope.
- The columns in the inserted and deleted tables correspond to the columns in the table that triggered the event.

What is a transaction and how is it used in SQL? Along with exception handling and error handling.

Transactions in SQL are a group of related database operations that are treated as a single unit. They are designed to ensure data integrity and consistency by guaranteeing that either all operations within a transaction are executed successfully or none of them are. This is known as the **ACID** principle (Atomicity, Consistency, Isolation, Durability).

Key Concepts of Transactions:

- **Atomicity:** A transaction is either executed entirely or not at all. If any part of the transaction fails, the entire transaction is rolled back to its original state.
- **Consistency:** The database must be in a consistent state before and after a transaction. This means that all constraints and rules are enforced.
- **Isolation:** Transactions should not interfere with each other. Each transaction should appear to be the only transaction running in the system.
- **Durability:** Once a transaction is committed, its changes are permanent and should survive system failures.

Using Transactions in SQL:

To use transactions in SQL, you typically enclose a group of SQL statements within a BEGIN TRANSACTION and COMMIT TRANSACTION block. If an error occurs during the transaction, you can use ROLLBACK TRANSACTION to undo all changes made within the transaction.

Exception handling and **error handling** are essential components of SQL transactions, ensuring data integrity and preventing unexpected failures.

Exception Handling:

- **Purpose:** Captures and manages errors that occur during transaction execution.
- **Mechanism:** Uses the TRY...CATCH block.

Example:

```
BEGIN TRY
   --Transaction logic
  BEGIN TRANSACTION;
  -- ...Other SQL statements
  COMMIT TRANSACTION;
END TRY
BEGIN CATCH
  --Error handling logic
  DECLARE @ErrorMessage NVARCHAR(MAX) =
ERROR_MESSAGE();
  DECLARE @ErrorNumber INT = ERROR_NUMBER();
```

```
  --Rollback the transaction if an error occurred
  ROLLBACK TRANSACTION;
  --Log the error or take other appropriate actions
  RAISERROR(@ErrorMessage, @ErrorNumber, 1);
END CATCH;
```

Error Handling:

- **Purpose:** Identifies and addresses potential errors that may occur during a transaction.
- **Techniques:**
  - RAISERROR: Raises a user-defined error message.
  - ERROR_MESSAGE() and ERROR_NUMBER(): Retrieve error details.
  - @@ERROR: Checks if an error occurred.
  - XACT_STATE(): Determines the transaction state.

Key Considerations:

- **Logging:** Log errors for analysis.
- **Rollback:** Rollback the transaction to prevent inconsistent data.
- **Retry Logic:** Consider retrying the transaction if appropriate.

Combining Exception Handling and Error Handling:

- Enclose transaction logic within a TRY...CATCH block.
- Use RAISERROR to provide custom error messages.

- Log errors for analysis and debugging.
- Implement rollback logic to maintain data integrity.
- Consider retrying the transaction if appropriate, but be cautious of infinite loops.

What is Savepoint in SQL Transaction?

Savepoints in SQL transactions allow you to mark specific points within a transaction. This enables you to partially roll back the transaction to a savepoint if an error occurs or if you need to undo certain changes while keeping others.

Example:

```
BEGIN TRANSACTION;

-- Insert a new customer

INSERT INTO Customers (CustomerID,CustomerName)

VALUES (1001, 'New Customer');

-- Create a savepoint

SAVE TRANSACTION sp1;

-- Insert an order for the new customer

INSERT INTO Orders (OrderID, CustomerID,OrderDate)

VALUES (10001, 1001, GETDATE());

-- If an error occurs here, you can roll back to sp1

IF ERROR_MESSAGE() IS NOT NULL

  ROLLBACK TRANSACTION savepoint_name;

COMMIT TRANSACTION;
```

In this example, a savepoint named sp1 is created after inserting the new customer. If an error occurs during the insertion of the order, the transaction can be rolled back to sp1, undoing the order insertion while keeping the customer insertion.

Key Points:

- Savepoints can be nested within transactions.
- You can create multiple savepoints within a transaction.
- Rolling back to a savepoint does not affect any changes made before the savepoint.
- Savepoints are only visible within the current transaction.

Use Cases for Savepoints:

- **Partial Rollback:** Undoing specific changes within a transaction while keeping others.
- **Error Handling:** Recovering from errors by rolling back to a previous state.
- **Complex Transactions:** Managing complex transactions with multiple steps.

What is a cursor and when is it used?

Cursors in SQL are used to process a result set one row at a time. They provide a way to iterate through the rows of a query result and perform operations on each individual row.

When to Use Cursors:

- **Row-by-Row Processing:** When you need to process each row of a result set individually, cursors are a good choice.
- **Complex Logic:** If you need to perform complex logic on

each row, cursors can provide more flexibility than set-based operations.

- **Modifying Data While Processing:** Cursors allow you to modify the data in a result set as you process it.

Types of Cursors:

- **Static Cursor:** The result set is fixed at the time the cursor is opened.
- **Keyset Cursor:** The result set is fixed, but updates to the underlying data can be seen.
- **Dynamic Cursor:** The result set can change during processing, allowing for additions, deletions, or modifications to the data.

Example:

```
DECLARE @CustomerID INT;

DECLARE @CustomerName VARCHAR(50);

DECLARE customer_cursor CURSOR FOR

SELECT CustomerID, CustomerName

FROM Customers;

OPEN customer_cursor;

FETCH NEXT FROM customer_cursor INTO@CustomerID, @CustomerName;

WHILE @@FETCH_STATUS = 0

BEGIN

  --Process the current row

  PRINT @CustomerID + ' - ' + @CustomerName;
```

```
--Update the customer
UPDATE Customers
SETCustomerName = 'Updated Customer'
WHERE CustomerID = @CustomerID;
FETCH NEXT FROM customer_cursor INTO @CustomerID, @CustomerName;
END
CLOSE customer_cursor;
DEALLOCATE customer_cursor;
```

In this example, a cursor is used to iterate through the Customers table, process each row, and update the customer name.

Important Considerations:

- **Performance:** Cursors can be less efficient than set-based operations for large result sets.
- **Complexity:** Using cursors can make your code more complex and harder to maintain.
- **Alternatives:** Consider using set-based operations or window functions whenever possible, as they are often more efficient.

CHAPTER 9

RESUME PREPARATION

In a job market characterized by an abundance of candidates possessing specific skill sets, how can individuals effectively differentiate themselves and capture the attention of recruiters to increase their visibility and job opportunities?

To navigate the complexities of today's job market, it's essential to understand the challenges recruiters face. With countless candidates competing for the same roles, standing out can be tough. Recruiters are inundated with applications, so making a quick and strong impression is crucial.

Ready to make a great first impression in your job search? Your resume is your golden ticket to capturing a potential employer's attention before you even say hello. It's your showcase, highlighting your skills and experiences.

A well-crafted resume can set you apart from the competition and increase more chances of getting called for an interview. But where do you start? What should your resume include? Don't worry, We're here to guide you step-by-step. Let's build a resume that wows!

What is Resume?

A Resume is a document with having concise summary of your professional experience, education, skills, and accomplishments. A resume plays an important role in a job placement.

What is a Curriculum Vitae or CV?

A Curriculum Vitae is a document that provides a complete overview of your academic, and professional qualifications, skills, and accomplishments. A CV plays an important role in applying for jobs in academic, research, scientific positions, or jobs outside India.

What is the difference between a Resume and a Curriculum Vitae (CV)?

A resume and a CV are different.

- **Resume:** A resume is a short summary of your work and education history. It's usually 2-3 pages long and focuses on the skills and experiences most relevant to a specific job.
- **CV:** A CV is a longer, more detailed document that includes everything about your work and education history. It can be 20, 30, or even more pages long. CVs are often used for academic or research jobs.

Another key difference is that CVs typically include references, while resumes usually don't.

Finally, you can tailor a resume for each job you apply for, but a CV is generally the same for every application.

What are the steps for preparing a great Resume?

Your outline is a solid foundation for building a resume. To make it even more effective, let's incorporate some additional key elements:

Steps for Preparing a Great Resume:

1. **Self-Assessment and Research:**
    - Identify your target job and industry.
    - Analyze job descriptions to understand required skills and

qualifications.

- Evaluate your strengths, weaknesses, and accomplishments.

2. **Choose the Right Resume Format:**
   - Determine the most suitable format (chronological, functional, or combination) based on your career history and target job.

3. **Create a Strong Header:**
   - Include your full name, professional title, phone number, email address, and LinkedIn profile (optional).
   - Consider adding a Professional profile picture for visual impact.

4. **Craft a Compelling Summary or Objective:**
   - Clearly articulate your career goals or highlight your key qualifications or experience.
   - Tailor this section to the specific job you're applying for.

5. **Highlight Skills:**
   - List both technical and soft skills.
   - Prioritize skills relevant to the job.
   - Consider using keywords from the job description.

6. **Showcase Your Experience:**
   - Use reverse chronological order to list your work history.
   - Quantify achievements with numbers and metrics whenever possible.
   - Use strong action verbs (achieved, managed, implemented) to start bullet points.

   - Tailor job descriptions to match the target job.

7. **Showcase Education:**
   - List degrees, certifications, and institutions attended.
   - Include relevant coursework or academic honors.
8. **Add Additional Sections (Optional):**
   - Include sections like projects, volunteer work, or awards if they add value.
9. **Proofread and Format:**
   - Ensure your resume is free of errors.
   - Use a clean, professional format with consistent fonts and spacing.
   - Consider using a resume builder tool for formatting assistance.
10. **Tailor and Optimize:**

- Customize your resume for each job application.
- Use keywords from the job description.

Additional Tips:

- **Keep it concise:** Aim for a one-page resume, unless you have extensive experience.
- **Use keywords effectively:** Incorporate keywords from the job description.
- **Highlight accomplishments:** Focus on results rather than just responsibilities.
- **Use a professional font and layout:** Choose a clean and easy-to-read format.

- **Proofread carefully:** Typos and grammatical errors can create a negative impression.

By following these steps and incorporating the additional tips, you can create a powerful resume that stands out from the competition.

Examples of career objectives for IT professionals

For Freshers Positions:

- Seeking a challenging IT position to leverage my [specific skills] and contribute to the organization's technological advancement while expanding my knowledge and expertise.
- To secure an entry-level IT role where I can apply my [skills] to deliver innovative solutions and drive business growth.

For Experienced Professionals:

- Results-oriented IT professional with [number] years of experience seeking a challenging role to optimize IT infrastructure and enhance operational efficiency.
- Seeking a leadership position in IT to oversee [specific area] and implement cutting-edge technologies to drive business success.

More Specific Examples (Based on Role):

- **Software Developer:** Seeking a software development position to create robust and scalable applications utilizing [programming languages] and contribute to innovative product development.
- **Network Engineer:** To obtain a Network Engineer position to design, implement, and maintain secure and efficient network infrastructures.
- **IT Support Specialist:** Seeking a role as an IT Support Specialist to provide exceptional technical assistance,

troubleshoot issues, and ensure optimal system performance.

What Hobbies shall I mention in your Resume?

From the below list, you can mention any one or two hobbies in your resume:

Hobbies that showcase transferable skills:

- **Learning languages:** Demonstrates adaptability and intellectual curiosity.
- **Playing a musical instrument:** Highlights discipline, focus, and teamwork (if in a band).
- **Volunteering:** Shows community involvement and empathy.
- **Public speaking or debating:** Demonstrates communication and leadership skills.
- **Coding or programming:** Relevant for tech-related roles.
- **Writing or blogging:** Indicates strong communication and creativity.
- **Photography or graphic design:** Highlights creativity and attention to detail.

Hobbies that showcase personality:

- **Traveling:** Demonstrates open-mindedness and adaptability.
- **Sports:** Shows teamwork, competitiveness, and physical fitness.
- **Reading:** Indicates intellectual curiosity and a love of learning.
- **Hiking or outdoor activities:** Suggests a healthy lifestyle and adventurous spirit.
- **Cooking or baking:** Demonstrates creativity and attention to detail.

If you're fresher then be prepared to answer any counter questions and elaborate more on mentioned hobbies in your resume. For experienced as well there are chances of discussion on hobbies so you should be prepared to answer for it.

Resume format for Fresher

[Your Name] [Your Pic(Optional)]

[Your Address] | [Your Email] | [Your Phone Number] | [LinkedIn Profile(Optional)] | [GitHub Profile(Optional)]

Objective

[Your Objective as per the job role]

Technical Skills

[Mention your technical skills point-wise in a group.]

For example: Web Technologies: HTML, CSS, JavaScript

Operating Systems: Linux, Windows

[Certifications (Optional)]

Education/Academic Excellence

[Your Degree, CGPA, Year of Passing]

[Your University Name, City, State]

[Relevant courses to this Job Role]

Projects

[Name of your project, Team Size]

[Your Role in this Project][Precise details of your project in points.]

[Internship Experience (Optional)

[Company name, city, state, From Month Year till Month Year]

Detailed experience in points]

[Academic Achievements (Optional)]

[Extracurricular Activities / Hobbies (Optional)]

[Details of GitHub Profile (Optional)]

Resume format for Experience

[Your Name] [Your Pic(Optional)]

[Your Address] | [Your Email] | [Your Phone Number] | [LinkedIn Profile(Optional)] | [GitHub Profile(Optional)]

Objective

[Your Objective as per the job role]

Technical Skills

[Mention your technical skills point-wise in a group.]

For example: Web Technologies: HTML, CSS, JavaScript

[Certifications (Optional)]

[Reverse Chronological Order of Experience]

[Company Experience]

[Company name, city, state, From Month Year till Month Year]

Projects

[Name of your project, Team Size]

[Your Role in this Project][Precise details of your project in points.]

Education/Academic Excellence

[Your Degree, CGPA, Year of Passing]

[Your University Name, City, State]

[Relevant courses to this Job Role]

[Academic Achievements (Optional)]

[Extracurricular Activities / Hobbies (Optional)]

[Details of GitHub Profile (Optional)]

LAND YOUR DREAM .NET JOB: DON'T WING YOUR INTERVIEW!

Are you a talented developer ready to take the next step in your career? .NET positions are booming, but competition is fierce. Don't gamble your future on outdated resources or winging the interview.

The ".NET Interview Preparation" Book is your one-stop shop for success. It's not just another question bank. This comprehensive guide dives deep into the essential knowledge you need to impress any interviewer.

Imagine confidently discussing:

- Software Development Life Cycle phases and best practices.
- .NET Framework concepts and its rich history.
- C# programming concepts like object-oriented programming.
- Utilizing powerful design patterns to create robust applications.
- Mastering essential collections in C# for efficient data management.
- Tackling exception handling with grace and clarity.
- Building powerful database interactions with ADO.NET and Entity Framework.

- Microsoft SQL Server understands the fundamentals.
- Crafting a winning resume that showcases your .NET expertise.

The ".NET Interview Preparation" Book equips you with the knowledge, confidence, and interview strategies to land your dream .NET job. Don't settle for anything less. Get your copy today!

Disclaimer

This book is for educational purposes only. Readers acknowledge that the author does not render legal, financial, medical, or professional advice. The content within this book has been derived from various sources. Please consult a licensed professional before attempting any techniques outlined in this book.

By reading this document, the reader agrees that under no circumstances is the author responsible for any direct or indirect losses incurred as a result of the use of the information contained within this document, including but not limited to errors, omissions, or inaccuracies.

Adherence to all applicable laws and regulations, including international, federal, state, and local governing professional licensing, business practices, advertising, and all other jurisdictions, is the sole responsibility of the purchaser or reader.

Neither the author nor the publisher assumes any responsibility or liability whatsoever on behalf of the purchaser or reader of these materials. Any perceived slight of any individual or organization is purely unintentional.

www.ingramcontent.com/pod-product-compliance
Ingram Content Group UK Ltd.
Pitfield, Milton Keynes, MK11 3LW, UK
UKHW062255290726
14090UKWH00017B/712